Beauty
AND THE
BEATS

Memoirs of a Female DJ

Beauty AND THE BEATS

Memoirs of a Female DJ

DJ SHY

iUniverse, Inc.

Bloomington

Beauty and the Beats
Memoirs of a Female DJ

Copyright © 2011 DJ Shy

iUniverse books may be ordered through booksellers or by contacting:

iUniverse
1663 Liberty Drive
Bloomington, IN 47403
www.iuniverse.com
1-800-Authors (1-800-288-4677)

Because of the dynamic nature of the Internet, any Web addresses or links contained in this book may have changed since publication and may no longer be valid. The views expressed in this work are solely those of the author and do not necessarily reflect the views of the publisher, and the publisher hereby disclaims any responsibility for them.

ISBN: 978-1-4620-0109-5 (pbk)
ISBN: 978-1-4620-0110-1 (ebk)

Library of Congress Control Number: 2011902611

Printed in the United States of America

iUniverse rev. date: 5/26/2011

To my mother, for her love, sacrifice, and strength.

To my father, for taking me to my roots.

To my brother, for showing me patience and forgiveness.

To my best friend, Top Shelf Don P, for his honesty and protection.

To my friends, who have supported me over the years.

In remembrance of my grandmother, Hannah Sung, who taught me to have faith.

CONTENTS

PREFACE

Who's the life of the party these days? The female DJ. Not only do we get to hang out with stars like *Jersey Shore*'s Pauly D, the Kardashians, and Lady Gaga, we get paid tens of thousands of dollars to spin at the hottest nightclubs around the world.

DJ Shy with MTV's *Jersey Shore* Pauly D – Photography by Carell Augustus

Without a DJ, there's no music; and without music, there's no party. The right music can make or break a party, and promoters, club owners, and stars alike know this. A DJ can get the crowd jumping up and down on the dance floor with an old school tune, or they can set a sultry mood for the party with some relaxing R&B songs.

DJs hold a highly coveted and influential position in the music world. Music producers and DJs are paramount to the success of hip-hop and pop music. They decide what songs will become hits by putting them on heavy rotation in the clubs and on the radio. DJs are also largely responsible for innovations in the last 10 years of dance music. House, techno, hip-hop, trance, electronica—these music genres would be nowhere without the DJ. DJs create and define what popular music is today, which drives sales in other retail industries such as clothing, footwear, energy drinks, and video games.

DJ Sophia Lin with Khloe & Kourtney Kardashian

DJ Mia from MTV's *America's Best Dance Crew* with Lady Gaga

My name is DJ SHY and I was the first female on-air mixer (or turntablist DJ) for the number-one Top 40 radio station in America, 102.7 KIIS FM in Los Angeles. This Clear Channel station has over 2.6 million listeners each week and features Ryan Seacrest as its morning host. I currently spin Top 40, rock, 80s, electro, reggae, R&B, and hip-hop at the hottest events throughout Hollywood and around the world.

It wasn't easy to get to where I am today. Getting screwed on payments. Drugs. Stalkers. Lies and many empty promises. This is just the beginning of what female DJs deal with when they enter the male-dominated music industry. If the audience doesn't boo you, club promoters cheat you on your pay, or worse, try to sleep with you.

Surviving the industry is rough as a woman, but it's even worse if you're naïve and soft-spoken like me. I got my name DJ SHY because I'm a little bashful around new people. Yet despite my quiet demeanor, I eventually climbed up the ladder by spinning for the toughest crowds – black hip-hop clubs in Hollywood.

DJ Shy photographed by Lisa Villasenor

A small-town girl from Pennsylvania, I was pretty innocent when I first got into deejaying. I had stars in my eyes when I moved to Tinseltown, and people took advantage of me time and time again. I barely noticed the drugs and prostitution at certain parties when I first started spinning. After surviving a drive-by in Compton and midnight stalkers, I grew to be a little wiser.

Though I was naïve in my early days, I have never backed down from what I want. I may speak softly, but I have an aggressive streak that doesn't let up when I've got my eyes set on something. Determination, belief in myself, and my passion for music have catapulted me to the top of the industry.

Many young people are told by their parents they shouldn't dream of being a pop star, rapper, actor, or dancer. Instead, they need to hit the books and pursue a stable career, like being a doctor, an accountant, or a lawyer. I decided to go against the grain. I definitely did not have the support from my family—my mother discouraged me from spinning, and I initially worked a corporate job after college to please her, even though I was spinning at night.

I hope to motivate and inspire others who want to live their dream too. Even if you long to be president of the United States, a star athlete, or the next Bill Gates, I want everyone who reads this book to realize their passion and potential despite the obstacles that lie before them. For me, deejaying is a passion and getting paid is a privilege. I want to share my secrets of success in hopes that others can achieve happiness and success in their lives too.

Chapter 1:

Starting from Scratch

My dad's silver Cadillac pulled up in the driveway and rolled to a stop. It was a warm summer day in 1988, and I was only nine years old. I ran to the window in hopes that my dad was going to get out of his car and come inside. But before I could see anything, my mom yelled at me.

"Get away from the window, Karen!" she said in a stern voice. "Don't look. He's got another woman with him."

I don't think I saw another woman, but before my mom pulled me away from the window, I did get a quick glimpse my dad. He was just sitting in the driveway, looking up at the house. It was like he was trying to see us. It had been a few months since he'd left our family.

Karen's Father Howard Beck

My dad did what few Koreans did. Against tradition, he left my mom, my younger brother John, and me and flew back to South Korea, never to come back. I had just finished the third grade, and we had only lived in Edison, New Jersey, for about a year since we left Charlotte, North Carolina. My dad was an engineer and worked for IBM. His company moved him around a lot, which is how we ended up in Edison, where all the kids in school were stuck in the same classroom all day long, even during lunch, because we didn't have a cafeteria. I found it weird—I had never been in a school that didn't have a cafeteria.

In school, I was introduced to the idea of divorce. My grade school teacher had talked about it once during class. I don't remember the lesson, but for some reason, what she said stuck in my mind—divorce was "the legal way to end a marriage." I thought that sounded so proper and official, like some kind of clean, easy solution to your problems.

I knew my parents fought here and there, but I had no idea what was really going on at that point. They screamed and yelled at each other in Korean. I had no clue why they were angry or what they were saying because I didn't understand the language. After one particularly bad fight with my dad, I crept into the living room to find my mom standing next to the television, which had been knocked to the floor. She was visibly upset—her whole face was red, and tears streamed down her cheeks. It frightened me to see her in tears. I had never seen her cry, so I tried to be helpful.

"Hey ma, do you know what a divorce is?" I piped up. I continued and recited what my teacher had said. I was at a complete loss of how to help. Instead of being grateful, my mom got angry. I was trying to be helpful, but I didn't know that if my parents got divorced, we would never live with my father again.

Karen with dog Princess

When Mom was angry, that was it. Once she decided she wanted a divorce, she didn't waste any time. My dad moved out of the house and they separated for a little while, but once the decision was made, there were no lawyers, desperate pleadings on the phone, or second thoughts. When my dad left the country, Mom said it was because he didn't want to pay child support.

Out of nowhere one night, Mom ordered my little brother John and me to start packing. We hurried around the house, throwing whatever would fit into suitcases. In our wake, we left behind a ton of furniture, kitchenware, and clothes. We barely had time to understand what was happening or say goodbye to our friends. Then Mom crammed me, John, and our family dog, a Yorkie named Princess, into our little Ford Escort station wagon. We were like sardines in an overstuffed tin can. It all happened so fast, and everything was a blur. We drove for a long time. I had no idea where we were going. I was so tired, so confused. I couldn't help but cry and whimper for a long time, while my mom drove for what seemed like all night. Eventually I cried myself to sleep. I had no idea my entire life was about to change. When I woke up, it was still dark, but we were at my Uncle Paul's house in New Castle, Pennsylvania. We were starting all over again from scratch.

• •

New Castle was much smaller than Edison. There was one main road, a tiny "downtown" area, one "mall" with all of maybe ten stores, and farms as far as the eye could see. The township, called Neshannock after the Native American phrase for "the land between two rivers," was pure rural Amish country. The parking lot at the grocery store had special spaces reserved for Amish buggies. The Ku Klux Klan met once a month at the courthouse in Wilmington, just a short drive over into the next town. The population was so white and the town so small that virtually every non-white person around was directly related to me. Even to this day, more than 98 percent of Neshannock's population is white.

Amish Buggies – Photography by Jenni Ripley

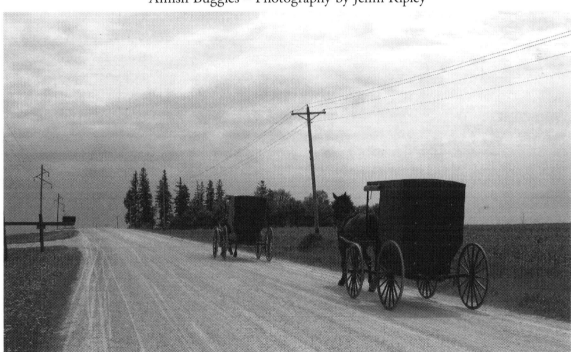

Uncle Paul was a doctor and he lived in the nice part of town. He, his wife, and their three children, Sarah, David, and Daniel, lived in a large, respectable house where weeping willows towered over the clean, wide street. All the other houses on the block were just like his—two-story structures with perfectly manicured lawns. Even though it was a really nice neighborhood, I immediately got a gut feeling that I was going to hate living there. In the past, my cousins had always ganged up on John and me because we were the youngest kids in the family. During our annual summer family vacations at Myrtle Beach in South Carolina, they would terrorize me, endlessly dunking my head underwater when I swam, stealing my salt water taffy, destroying my sand castles, and just bullying me all around. I couldn't believe that I had to live with them and endure their antics every day. My mother never indicated how long we would be staying with them. For a ten-year-old kid like me, this was a disaster!

My mom's brother was kind. Uncle Paul had his own family practice, providing the sick and elderly with the highest quality of medical care. As if we were his patients, he knew how to treat us well. He assured my mom that everything would be alright. He told us not to worry, that he understood our situation and would help us get back on our feet. My aunt, though, had other ideas. Being the Korean wife of a successful doctor meant she was queen of the household, if not all of New Castle, in her mind. Behind my uncle's back, she insisted we pay rent. My mom had no choice but to obey her.

Like many Koreans, I was raised in a Christian family. We attended my aunt and uncle's Korean church in nearby Youngstown, Ohio. Teeming with doctors and successful storeowners, it was a pretty wealthy congregation. Being one of the few Korean churches around, churchgoers from cities far away in East Ohio and West Virginia all congregated there. Everyone was really welcoming at first, but as soon as gossip spread that Mom was divorced and we were poor, things started to change.

In Korean culture, divorce is taboo. Couples are not supposed to divorce. Korean men who divorce their wives bring shame to their families, but it's almost worse to be the divorced woman with kids to care for. The exclusion and prejudice that we faced at the church weren't blatant. No one told us that they didn't want us around to my mom's face. It was much more subtle. Everyone except us would be invited to different social functions, like weddings, birthday parties, sleepovers, and movies. My mother and brother soon stopped attending church altogether. If it weren't for the encouragement, involvement, and persuasion of my bible study teachers, I would've stopped attending as well. Overall, we were outcasts who almost naturally fell into this social standing. I started to wonder where my father was. I don't think I fully realized what had happened. I mean, how could a ten-year-old like me truly understand the seriousness of our situation?

• •

Karen's mother Wendy Beck, 2ⁿᵈ from left

My mom, Won Soon, is a determined woman. She was born March 5, 1950, in Kyungki-Do, South Korea, a province that almost completely surrounds the nation's capitol, Seoul. She was born just a few months before North Korean forces sent a bomb into South Korea, launching the start of the Korean War. It was a difficult time. The country was split in two, and Koreans were fighting against each other. Many families were separated before the war started and are still trying to reunite with loved ones to this day. This is the chaos in which my mom was raised. I think living in a war made my mom particularly tough. Even though she was young and grew up humble without a father, she managed to persevere and become a registered nurse.

When it came time to find work, many of my mom's classmates left for other countries with the promise of better opportunities, especially the United States. There was an abundance of nursing jobs in America, so my mom followed suit and moved to Philadelphia in the summer of 1975 all by herself, hoping to find a better life.

Back then, Korean women were to be wed around the age of 25. At this point, Mom was already 27 and she definitely felt the pressure to get married. After a year or so of working in the States, Mom returned to Korea to go on a blind date with a bright, young engineering student. That's when she met my father, Huhn Soon Baik. A family member introduced my mom to my father and just three short months later, they got married.

Niagra Falls 1979

Like many Koreans who moved to the U.S., my father wanted us to fit in with the rest of Americans. He decided to change our Korean names to more American-sounding ones. My father changed his own to Howard. My mom became Wendy. I was born in America, but my parents had always called me by my Korean name, Jin Baik, for as long as I could remember. Then one day in first grade, I went to sit down at my usual desk at school but was surprised to see someone else's nametag on it. "This is my desk! Who is Karen Beck?" I asked my teacher. My teacher explained that my father had legally changed my name. I hated my new name Karen. It sounded like "carrot."

Mom worked as a nurse in two nursing homes before settling down as a housewife to take care of my brother and me. But when my dad left and Mom was desperate for money, she decided to open her own business. Even though she had to pay her sister-in-law rent and barely spoke English, she somehow found a way to secure a loan and open up a small retail shop. To name her store, we flipped through baby name books for an idea. It didn't take long. We didn't want to name it Wendy's because we didn't want people to confuse her store with the fast food restaurant. Instead, Mom decided on "Darlene's" because it sounded like "darling."

Mom found a small space in the Towne Mall in New Castle to set up shop. She sold women's accessories—all sorts of cheap fanciful purses, jewelry, hair accessories, and wigs—from 9 in the morning until 6 or even 7 o'clock at night. Once a month, she would leave New Castle on a Saturday and drive all night—a brutal seven hours—to Flushing, Queens, in New York City, and then catch the morning train to Manhattan to stock up on wholesale merchandise. She'd spend the day buying her wares, and then she would drive all the way back on Sunday evening so she could open up shop Monday morning again.

Mom shouldered all of the store's duties herself. She spent most of her time alone, working nine or ten hours a day, six days a week. She didn't hire extra help in order to save money. People would come in and shoplift, but she let them get away with it because she spoke English poorly and feared they might harass or rob her later. Her brothers complained and scolded her, saying she worked too hard and reminding her that she had two little children to watch over. They doubted her ability to run a store and raise two children all by herself. But my mom was determined to make ends meet and to stop relying on my uncle's kindness. She wanted us to get back on our feet as soon as possible.

In just six months, Mom saved up enough money to buy our own place on Sankey Lane, a small street with a few houses. My brother and I were relieved to leave my uncle's house at last, away from our bullying cousins and resentful aunt. Our new house was a brown, single-story unit that was long and narrow, with a gravel driveway. It was a trailer home, but it was all our own, and the backyard was full of woods and streams that I could spend hours exploring by myself.

• •

Karen's elementary class in Charlotte, NC

My life before New Castle was very different. I grew up in Charlotte, North Carolina, where I attended preschool all the way through second grade. Charlotte was an urban city with a mix of white, black, Hispanic, and Asian populations. In my class alone, I remember a Vietnamese girl, a Puerto Rican kid, a couple of black kids, and me, a Korean. Everybody got along. We even used to chant that playground rhyme, "Chinese, Japanese, dirty knees. Look at these" together, all of us laughing and pulling back our eyelids to look "chinky." We had no idea that it was offensive or politically incorrect; we just thought it was funny. I even showed my mom.

Those days in North Carolina were filled with interesting and funny moments that I still remember. As a kid, I was naturally outgoing and adventurous. Unlike other kids, I didn't cry when my mom dropped me off for preschool. I saw the toys and made a beeline toward my target. I liked to do my own thing and had little fear. I climbed trees and played with Legos and Transformers. Fussing with a Barbie was not my style.

Every summer, the University of North Carolina hosted an international festival. One year, my mom participated by performing a solo traditional Korean fan dance. It was such a big deal back in those days that the local news covered her performance. Seeing her up there on stage stirred something in me. Trying to emulate my mother, I spotted an empty stage that had a working microphone. Even though we were leaving, I broke away from my parents, ran to the mic, and brazenly belted out my ABCs to a captive and startled audience. I was three years old. I thought I was a star. After I finished, I walked off the stage like it was nothing; just another day in the life of Karen Beck.

International Festival at the University of North Carolina

I was the kid who walked right up to strangers and easily made new friends. Once, when we were standing in line at the grocery store behind a large man and his wife, I walked up to them, poked the man in the stomach, and sweetly asked him when his baby was due. My mom was mortified, but the man's wife just laughed. I wasn't shy with boys either. I had lots of crushes and let the boys know it, even at five years of age. I had a strategy: Call a boy over, pretend like I was going to tell him a secret, and then—smooch! Plant a big, wet kiss on his ear.

I considered myself a trendsetter, but I hated when people would copy me or follow my lead. Throughout grade school, I exhibited a fierce sense of individuality and independence. I wanted to know and experience everything. When someone replicated my idea, it made me angry, forcing me to find another way to brand something my own. If I had to draw a dog for art class and the girl next to me was copying how I drew the tail, paws, or eyes, I would crumple the paper, toss it out, and make a different one. When a teacher asked me to read aloud from a storybook, instead of merely reading the words, I would enlist different voices and create characters to make it interesting. I had to be different. I had to stand out. I credit grade school for developing my creative streak. I loved expressing myself through music and art. I tried piano lessons and instantly took to it.

Karen on the piano

So many of my childhood afternoons were spent playing music and singing at the top of my lungs. Little did I know that in high school, all this would change. Suddenly, playing piano and having a penchant for singing gave people license to shun you. It just wasn't cool.

• •

Fortunately, my introduction to Neshannock Elementary was a welcoming one. On the first day of fourth grade, I instantly became "popular." Everyone thought I was like Claudia Kishi, the Japanese girl in the Baby-sitter's Club, a book series that was a favorite of girls everywhere in the '80s. These books were a big deal with the girls in my school. One time, I boarded the school bus with John and our cousin Daniel. It was packed. The boys found seats up front. Just as I was about to sit down next to them, a girl called my name from the back of the bus. Her name was Crystal Norris, and she invited me to sit with her. Daniel, who was a year older than me, was dumbfounded. According to him, no one was ever invited to sit with the popular kids in the "exclusive" back seats of the school bus.

As the popularity of Baby-sitter's Club diminished and we grew older, my classmates began to place more value on the "haves and have-nots". This meant fitting in would prove harder as I got older, and things would change for the worst. Our financial woes would eventually cost me my friends and, more importantly, my self-esteem.

· ·

Since my mom was frugal, we could only afford to watch regular television—no cable. We only got three television channels: NBC, CBS, and ABC. Sometimes, if we had good reception, we also had PBS. My brother and I were constantly fiddling with the antennas so we could get a better picture. One of us would get all sweaty moving those pointy rabbit ears around while the other stood by, frustrated at the static on the TV screen. With just three TV channels and public broadcast at my reach, I was pretty out of touch with the rest of the world. I watched cartoons and shows like *Quantum Leap* and *Dr. Quinn, Medicine Woman*. I also watched *Saved by the Bell* on Saturday mornings, which was the hippest show I knew of. Fashion, hair, make-up, pop culture—it was all a mystery to me. I knew nothing about what was considered cool back then. I didn't wear any make-up; all my clothes were hand-me-downs from my male cousins. People at school made fun of how I dressed, especially since my clothes were mostly boys' clothes. I wore Velcro sneakers only once when I started high school—until the boys pointed and laughed. I didn't dare let on the fact that my parents were divorced, on top of everything else. I figured those kids had enough ammunition.

My childhood was filled with friends of almost every color, but my high school years were an entirely different story. At Neshannock Junior Senior High School, the economic, racial, and social divide between my church, family, and friends became very clear. Almost overnight, friends started obsessing over clothes and favorite TV shows—I was completely out of sync. I didn't have a clue. Mötley Crüe were foreign words to me. It was the same story at church. Kids I had been friends with all along were suddenly talking about things that I didn't know anything about. Who were the New Kids on the Block? Why was the number 90210 so special? I couldn't name any trendy clothing brands like Banana Republic, French Connection, or Nautica. We hardly shopped for clothes; we never had any money to do so. The first time I can remember Mom taking me shopping was during high school. We went to a third-rate outlet store called Value City. Thanks to cable television, my friends experienced a brighter, slicker, hipper world, while I remained hopelessly in the dark.

Sometimes our differences were subtle. Once, during music class, we were given a couple of new songs to sing. Being an avid music lover, I did my best to learn them. I sang along happily, belting out every note, completely ignorant to the fact that none of my friends, the popular crowd, were doing the same. Out of the corner of my eye, I saw that they were just sitting around, not really paying attention. Confused, I asked them why weren't they singing. They smiled and said they just didn't feel like it. I felt my cheeks go red. I realized then that my friends—and the rest of my peers—did not deem musical creativity cool. I felt like a total moron and pretended not to care about singing either. Fitting in was more important.

Other times, our differences were clear as day. I invited a friend over to my house to hang out. Her dad, a wealthy doctor, had promised to drop her off at my house after school. When I saw their car pull up, I ran out to the front lawn and started waving so they wouldn't miss my house. My friend's dad slowed the car down. I could see him glaring through the windshield at me and my trailer home. I watched as they just kept right on driving until the car was a tiny speck in the distance. It was almost accusatory, the way her dad looked at me, as if to say "How dare you think you're good enough to play with my daughter?" I felt smaller and smaller as they drove away.

Sadly, it was no different for my mom. When she had enough money to move us out of our trailer home, my mom hired a real estate agent to help find a new house in a nicer neighborhood. But very soon it became clear that some sellers were opposed to the idea of a minority buying and enjoying their house. Mom was refused many showings. The real estate agent was so embarrassed and kept apologizing. But Mom did not let any of it bother her. She was determined to buy a better house.

She eventually did. Our next house was two whole stories, just like my uncle's. I was so happy to move, not only because the house and neighborhood were an upgrade, but also because the area was full of people from school. My friend, Brooke Wacikowski, lived across the street. I felt less isolated. Maybe things would change for the better, I thought. But whatever sense of hope I carried with me after our move, it did not last long.

Our house was located on the corner of a busy intersection. That made it a surefire target for vandalism; it was like it had a bright red bull's eye on it. Broken eggs on the car, tire marks on the lawn, toilet paper in the trees—my family was too embarrassed to clean it up. Our prized "home, sweet home" would sit humiliated for weeks. Neighborhood kids even started setting off firecrackers around our house—the big ones with sparks and shooting flames. Unlucky for us, New Castle is known as the fireworks capital of America, so there were plenty of pyrotechnics to go around. The city might as well have fully endorsed terrorizing my family. One time, I was greeted at the door by an exploding firecracker. What would have happened had I stuck my head out just a little farther? It's not a pleasant thought.

The cops got to know our family pretty well during those years. Every time something happened, they would come and fill out a police report. As I got older, my mom became stricter with me. My curfew was an unforgivable 6 o'clock. If I showed up even a minute late, my mom would report that I was missing to the police. So many times, I came home to a scene in the living room where officers would be talking to my mom. She and I would immediately launch into an argument in front of them. My brother John, on the other hand, seemed unable to do any wrong. Not only did he not have a curfew, he was also given the choice of who he wanted to hang out with, while my mom and I constantly argued over my choice of friends.

As my friends started to drop off and I became more and more of a social outcast, I drew into myself more. To keep myself busy, I hit the books hard and studied. To keep myself from feeling bored, I threw myself into school activities. Besides playing the clarinet, I joined science and social clubs and participated in many sports. Even though I wasn't all that religious, I attended many church retreats just to get out of the house. On the weekends, I volunteered at the local hospital. During the summer, I signed up with the soccer league for the predominantly Amish school in Wilmington because my school didn't have a soccer program. Even though I was the only girl on an all boys team, I started as a left fullback. I was so proud; I wanted my mom to see me play before the season was over. I kept asking her to come, but she was always too busy. It finally came down to our last game of the season, and again, she could not take time off from the store. There was just no one else that she could rely on to cover for her. While everyone else's parents cheered their kids on, I was once again left alone. Our team won the title of champions of our league that year. I was pretty happy about it, but deep down I was disappointed that my mom was unable to come to any games to see me win. What I didn't realize back then was that she was a very dedicated parent. All the times she told me she couldn't come to my soccer games, she was busy running her own business without help or support to give my brother and me a better life. She drove us to school every day, from the time I was in middle school until I turned 16. It's no wonder we both had perfect attendance throughout all those years.

• •

In high school, all the joy I had as a child left me. Being trapped at home; losing my friends; enduring vandalism and teasing; fights with my brother and arguments with my mom—all of it just made me feel different from everybody else. I hated being poor, being a minority, being locked down with a curfew, and not having a dad. Though John and I talked to my dad every once in a while, he was, for the most part, out of the picture. He never gave my mom a penny in child support. Even to this day, none of us really ever talk about their divorce.

My family was different in so many ways, in every social circle we were a part of—at school, church, even among our own extended family. On the surface, I pretended like everything was okay, like I was just any other busy teenager trying to get through school and make it into college. But beneath the serene surface, I was like a pot of boiling water. At home, my anger would find an outlet in my younger brother John. I abused him to no end, physically and mentally degrading him in every imaginable way. I belittled him, bossed him around, and even got violent when he failed to give in to my demands. When he did something as insignificant as refusing to make me a milkshake, I rammed my fist into his bedroom door, punching a hole in it. My mom worried and asked my cousin to supervise us. My outbursts were getting extreme, and I was just so angry at everything and everyone. But outside my home life, nobody was the wiser. I would just bottle up all of my frustrations and play the quiet, good Christian student at school.

I needed another outlet for my feelings. As soon as I got a car, I started stealing. One day, I drove my new Geo Metro all the way to neighboring Ohio, to a department store in the Southern Park Mall. I just wanted to look at clothes, to maybe pretend I was rich, or try to feel what it must be like to be able to go to the store and buy whatever I wanted without any worry about money for once. It took about an hour to get there and I remember being antsy the whole way. I pulled into a parking spot and walked in. Immediately, I was enveloped by crowds of people walking around leisurely, like they didn't have a care the world. There was pleasant music playing in the background. I felt out of place. I walked into one of the department stores and saw endless racks of clothes. It was like everything I ever wanted, so close and yet so out of reach. I glanced at the price tags and something came over me. I grabbed a bunch of items and headed for the changing room. Without thinking, I ripped off the tags, made sure there were no sensors, and quickly put them on under my clothes. As I was walking out, I felt like everyone was staring at me, like they knew. I tried to act normal, but my heart was racing. When I got out of the store, I let out a big breath and a rush of happiness flooded over me. It was like a high. I had never felt that way before. I got clothes for free, and that made me feel so incredibly good. I shoplifted a few more times after that, but each time, the high failed to last as long as the time before. The excitement of having new clothes, of posing as someone else—gaining a new identity—quickly wore off. It didn't matter what clothes I was wearing on my back. Underneath, I was still the same poor Asian girl who came from a broken home. No matter what I did, I still felt inferior.

Chapter 2:
Lockdown

I began my freshman year of high school in the fall of 1993 just as I did the fourth grade in New Castle—unsure of myself and somewhat timid. This time, however, there was no one to rescue me from my isolation. No one called out to me from the back of the bus, no one invited me to sit down next to them. I hovered around the edges, feeling invisible. Neshannock Junior Senior High School only had about 100 students per grade. Because our school was small, the social divisions were somewhat blurred. The world of cheerleaders would overlap a little with the band, and athletes mingled with some academic types. Within those intersections, though, there was always another inner circle where social hierarchies were more pronounced. It was kind of like a celebrity-hosted Hollywood party. You think that just because you're there, you're "in," but then you realize that all the real celebrities are behind velvet ropes in the VIP room, and everyone else around you is just like you—pretty average and feeling kind of foolish, as if you're all putting on some charade. I floated around in the fringes of these circles. In the hallways and at lunch I said hi to band nerds, geeks, and some jocks, but I never really sat down and made friends with any of them.

Jennifer DiLorenzo & Karen Beck

My one friend was Jennifer DiLorenzo. Jennifer lived about five minutes from my house, and we were in band together. We rode our bikes all over the neighborhood, grew very close, and chatted about everything. I really looked forward to hanging out with her after school—it made me feel like I finally had a best friend. She confessed that she had a secret crush on Jake Marshall to me. A tall, slim Italian American, Jake played the drums with us in band. He had the dark, handsome looks and charismatic smile of a teen heartthrob. But even as Jennifer divulged all her deep, dark secrets about her obsession with Jake Marshall, I knew he had a crush on me. It was in the way he looked at me during band class. My stomach would flip, and I couldn't help but smile when he was around.

My mom never talked to me about sex. The Neshannock Township school system didn't offer any sex ed classes either. I never saw that old film reel about the birds and the bees in a darkened classroom full of snickering kids. When it came to the rules of attraction, I was totally out of the game. All I knew about sex was that you weren't supposed to talk about it. And if you did talk about it, you were a bad, unrepentant sinner. That's the message I got in church.

I remember the first time I came across one of these "bad" people. I was home one night, hanging out in my room before dinner when the phone rang. I ran to answer it and heard a male voice on the other end.

"Is this Karen?"

"Yes," I answered, uneasily, not recognizing the voice.

"This is Mike," he said. "I saw you at the football game. I go to Laurel High School." I had no idea who he was or how he got my phone number, but before I could say anything, he blurted out all these sexual things. My face went hot. I felt like some creepy man had just opened his trench coat and exposed himself to me. My first reaction was swift. I started yelling at him about how he needed God and Christianity. I was convinced the devil had gotten a hold of Mike and was forcing him to behave in such an evil way. Preaching to him was the only defense I knew. In the middle of my religious tirade, my mom's voice came bellowing out to me from another room, "Karen! Hang up the phone! Hang up right now!"

This one time was a welcome interruption, but usually Mom's eavesdropping was cause for discord in our relationship. She'd been listening in on my phone calls since I started high school. I'd hear tiny clicks while I was talking, and then the phone line would sound a little a hollow, like the faintest breeze in my ear. She'd always interrupt my conversations at crucial moments too, like if someone mentioned a party or a boy. Suddenly I'd hear her yelling at me to get off the phone or claiming that my brother needed to make a call.

My mom and I fought a lot back in those days. Most of the time she was angry and yelling at me. My mom became very strict. We battled to no end, and I just didn't get it. Now, looking back, I guess it was because she was a single mom and felt she needed to keep a tight reign on her kids. It didn't help that she couldn't speak English very well and was raised in traditional Korean culture. Maybe she had heard some stories about American teenagers who disobeyed their parents and got into all kinds of trouble. Maybe she was a little freaked out without my dad to help her parent. She wanted to know where I was, what I was doing, and whom I was doing it with, 24 hours a day, seven days a week. It didn't even feel like she worked full time because it seemed like her eyes and ears were always all around me. I felt her presence at home, at school, everywhere. She acted more like a jail warden than a mom. It didn't help that my curfew was 6 o'clock on the nose, or basically whenever she came home, which some days could be as early as 5:30. She never told us she was coming home early, or even a little late for that matter. Making us guess was her way of keeping us honest. We always had to make sure we were home on time, just in case she happened to be there already. Sometimes, though, it was hard to keep track all the time. Especially when you had a boyfriend.

Jake Marshall asked me to be his girlfriend out of the blue one day. It happened over the phone. I hardly ever talked to him, but without hesitation I said yes. He was undeniably cute, and you couldn't argue with that. Jennifer stopped talking to me, but I didn't care. He was my first kiss.

Jake was a year older than me. When he started telling people that we were dating, I wore it like a badge of honor. It was like he was telling everyone, "Hey, this girl is cool." Kids at school started coming up to me and asking if the rumors were true. It felt so good to say yes. For once, other people accepted me. I was extremely proud of our relationship. I felt like a person. I had an identity. I guess back then that was more important to me then than my friendship with Jennifer. My mom didn't see it that way, though. Instead of being a little bit happy about it or even just talking to me about it, she got a very serious look on her face when I broke the news to her.

"No, no," she said slowly, shaking her head. "No boyfriend. Just friend. Only STUDY!" And that was the end of the conversation.

I didn't care what Jennifer or my mom said. Jake and I would hang out during lunch and whenever we had a chance during school. Jake's best friend Sean was a junior and the only child of a nurse. He had a car and a driver's license, so after school, Jake and I would pile into Sean's car and cruise around town, talking and hanging out.

One day after school, Jake got the idea to hang out at Sean's house since his Mom was always busy working at the hospital. I had some time before my 6 o'clock curfew, even if my mom came home a little early, so I agreed. When we got to his house, I felt butterflies in my stomach. We were all hanging out in the living room, listening to music. Jake was making me laugh and looking at me *that* way. I felt like I could stay there forever. Everything felt right, like the way things were supposed to be. I didn't think about tomorrow or even about later that night; I only thought about the moment and how good it felt to be wanted. I wanted so badly to stay a little longer, to make that feeling last. I kept pushing it. 5:30 came and went, then 5:45. I knew I needed to get home, but something made me stay.

We finally left at 6 o'clock. We were just driving up to my house when I saw a police car in the driveway. My heart jumped. The boys got really quiet. Sean slowed the car down, and I felt the blood drain from my face. They asked if everything was alright. I told Sean to drop me off just a block before my house. I tried to brush it off. I said everything was fine, not to worry. I got out of the car and told Jake I'd talk to him later, then watched them drive away.

As I walked up the driveway, my mind was racing. I could see that the front door was open slightly. My mom, her face all contorted, was sitting on the couch, talking to a policeman who was taking notes in a big black notepad. When I pushed open the door my mom bolted upright. She immediately started screaming at me in Korean. She'd called the cops because I wasn't home and she didn't know where I was. I was so embarrassed. One of the officers tried to calm her down, while the other asked me all sorts of questions. My head was spinning. I didn't know who to listen to. I started screaming back at her, "Why did you call the cops?" which just made her yell louder. She was furious, but so was I. My mom demanded to know where I was. I stammered that I was at my friend's house. She wanted to know which one and started walking toward the phone. I knew I was doomed, so I told her the truth.

The cops closed their notepads and left us to take care of our own troubles. During all this, the sun had gone down outside, and nighttime settled. My mother and I just faced each other in the darkened living room, both of our faces red with anger and frustration.

We stood there for what seemed like hours, as if we were in a stand-off. In rapid-fire Korean, my mom yelled at me about throwing my life away, getting pregnant, having no future. I had no idea where she was getting all these ridiculous ideas. How would I get pregnant when nothing had even happened between me and Jake? But my mom was stubborn, and she wasn't going to let up until I agreed to break up with Jake. My whole body was burning with outrage. Life was so unfair! Why couldn't I live a normal teenage life like everyone else? I was convinced that everything would've been different if my dad were around. I knew *he* would understand. "I want to live with Dad," I yelled at my mom. "Why couldn't I live with him?" She didn't answer, but I could tell that just those words alone stung.

• •

My mom didn't want to have anything to do with my dad. After he moved back to Korea, he tried to reconnect with my brother John and me to establish some kind of presence in our lives. Maybe he was trying to carve out a role for himself in our family, even though he was no longer a part of it. Through the years, he found out where we lived and would write letters telling us about Korea, asking how we were. Sometimes he'd send us packages of little souvenirs, like silver spoons inscribed with details about a different city or region of Korea. Every time my mom found his postcards or souvenirs in our rooms, she'd throw them all away.

Postcard from Dad

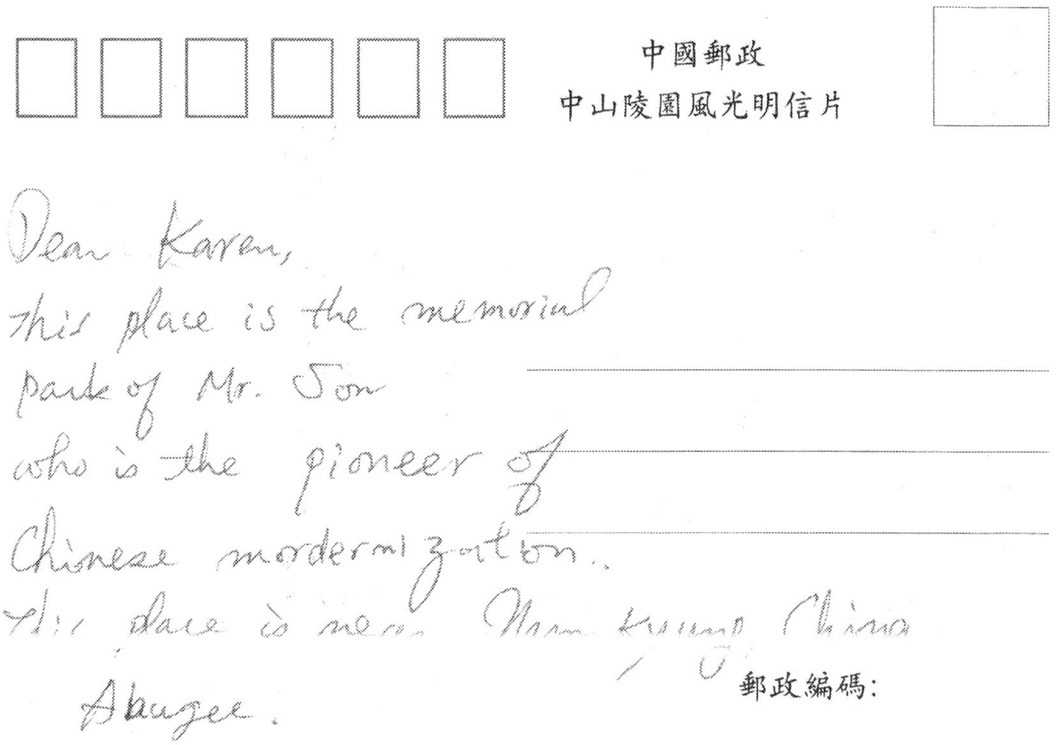

中國郵政
中山陵園風光明信片

郵政編碼：

Dear Karen,
this place is the memorial
park of Mr. Son
who is the pioneer of
Chinese mordernization..
This place is new Nan kyung China
Abugee.

My dad was never an emotional man. He was tall for a Korean, about 6 feet, with a serious expression and dark features. People said he looked Filipino. A lot of people said I looked more like him than my mom. My dad was not the hugging type. Perhaps this was due to the fact that as a child in Korea, he had been living as an orphan. He never kissed us, unlike my mom, who was constantly scooping us up in her arms and showering us with kisses when we were children. He had an almost paranoid fear of germs. When we lived in Charlotte, one of my classmates invited all the girls in our class for a birthday sleepover party at her house. My dad refused to let me go because he was afraid of all the germs I might bring home. He was diligent about checking our mouths to make sure my brother and I brushed our teeth properly. He always seemed tightly wound up, so I constantly looked for ways to make him laugh, or at least smile a little. I did silly things and put on impromptu shows for him. He would smile and grab my nose and I would giggle, happy that my dad seemed alright just then. I thought, if my dad were around, all I'd have to do is make him smile and everything would be fine. With my dad around, I knew how to make things better.

As the weeks went by, defying my mom to see Jake got more and more difficult. She was on my case about everything—where I was, whom I was with. I began to realize that being in a relationship was just unrealistic, especially with my mom's unreasonable rules and expectations. I decided the only way to cut myself some slack at home was to end it with Jake. Once I made the decision in my mind, it was easy to break up. I simply walked up to Jake one day at lunch and told him in front of all his friends that we would just be friends, then walked away. Just like that, all the status and feelings of belonging I'd gained by being Jake's girlfriend faded away, but I felt relieved—like a huge weight had been lifted from my shoulders. Luckily for me, Jennifer and I had slowly become friends again, even though I'd stabbed her in the back. But our friendship wasn't the same as before. We weren't as close, but I was happy for the little bit I got.

• •

I don't remember when it started, but my dad started calling us at home. It was never when my mom was around. She didn't know that he contacted us. Our phone conversations were always a little awkward, wavering between happiness and anxiety. I loved hearing the sound of his voice, but I always felt a little removed from it. He was my father, but I didn't know this man. It was like I was talking to a poor, lonely stranger on the phone.

One day, he called and said he was in America. He wanted to see us, but my mom couldn't know, so my brother and I planned for him to come by our house on a Saturday when my mom was working. He said he would take us out to lunch. I spent the entire morning that day cleaning the house from top to bottom. As the hour approached, we ran to the front window at the sound of every car, surveying the street to see if he had arrived. I was so afraid he would be late, or worse, he wouldn't show up. After what seemed like hours, we heard a car pull up to the driveway. I ran to the window and saw an Asian man get out. He was alone. I rushed to the door and opened it. My brother John and I stood there for a few moments, not really knowing what to do. I gave him a quick hug, and he patted me on the back. John and I were excited. We quickly brought him inside and showed him around the house. I remember he looked impressed, like he didn't think that my mom would have done as well as she had. Lunch felt weird. I felt like I was sitting with a distant relative, but I felt a strong tug toward him. It had been five years since I last saw him. He looked so much older. I realized that I did too.

After the short visit, my dad continued to write and call every once in a while. But once we all got email, communication got a thousand times easier. He started visiting us more often, once or twice a year. Our regular meeting spot turned out to be the very mall where my mom's store was. John and I would usually visit her on the weekends and spend time at the other end of the mall in the television department of Sears to catch up on some cable. Dad would wait for us there, and mom would never know.

My dad wanted us to come visit him in Korea. We'd never been. He told us how beautiful it was and about all the places he wanted to take us. One day, I found a letter in the mailbox from him, and inside were two tickets to Korea—one for me and the other for John. I was so excited; I'd never been on a plane before. Not thinking, I ran to my mom and showed her the tickets. Without hesitation, she grabbed them and ripped the tickets into pieces. Immediately, she began snooping through my belongings where she eventually found a stash of letters and gifts from my dad. I begged for them back but they all ended up in the trash. It was quite clear we were to have nothing to do with him. Maybe she thought he might kidnap us. I didn't care.

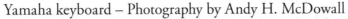

After I broke up with Jake Marshall, life at my house calmed down a lot. I fell into a regular schedule, coming straight home after class and studying diligently, while my brother locked himself in his room with his computer. Life was pretty mundane. I spent my energy learning how to play different instruments. Some days I'd go over to the music store to get supplies. One time, I headed over there to get a new reed for my clarinet when I laid my eyes on this beautiful, amazing keyboard.

Yamaha keyboard – Photography by Andy H. McDowall

It was a Yamaha PSR-630 MIDI keyboard with a computer built into it, so you could record music as you played. I thought it was so dope and I immediately wanted it. But a MIDI tag for $700, I was so disappointed. I went home feeling dejected; it seemed so out of reach, but I couldn't stop thinking about it. The keyboard was always on my mind. At school, I'd imagine all the music I could create with it. When I got home, I'd pretend the piano was a keyboard, but it just wasn't quite the same. I moped around the house, wishing I had that keyboard. I'd never wanted something so bad.

I tried to forget about the keyboard and kept myself busy with band, school, and volunteering. Friday nights when the band played at football games were the highlight of my week—it was the only time I ever got out of the house after hours. Since my mom worked, I sometimes got a ride to and from the games with a fellow bandmate who my mom knew. On the night of the big homecoming game, you could just feel the excitement in the air at school. My friend Michelle Janovich asked if I wanted to go to Perkin's, a greasy spoon diner, after the game. Perkin's was not only the one 24-hour restaurant in town, it was *the* hangout for teenagers. I had only been to Perkin's during the day when it was mainly filled with retirees and senior citizens, but the night after the big game, Perkin's promised to be the prime social event of the semester. I begged my mom to let me go, and surprisingly she agreed, on the condition that I called her precisely at 11 o'clock so she could pick me up.

By the time we arrived that night, Perkin's parking lot was already packed with cars. Inside it was so loud and crowded that we had to squeeze ourselves through dozens of people to get to our table. The restaurant was a sea of colors from kids' letterman jackets. There were reds, blacks, whites, blues—all from different schools in the other townships of New Castle, including our own. Laughter and excited chatter filled the restaurant, and we had to shout our orders to our waitress and across the table to hear each other. My eyes were wide from all the sights and sounds. It was warm inside and I felt accepted, like someone was giving me a big hug.

That night, I felt like I was in my element. By nature, I'm an extremely social person, and with football fervor buzzing around me at Perkin's, I shed my outcast awkwardness just for a moment. It felt good, even comfortable. While I may have looked like my dad, my mom's social nature was definitely passed on to me. When we were little, my mom was always the outgoing and smiling one, quick to laugh and make friends. Like her, I loved being around people and hated to be alone. Even today, I can't live in my house alone. I need roommates to make me feel truly at home. So even though some of my friends were getting antsy that night because it was taking forever for our food to arrive, I didn't mind at all. I was riding on the high of the game, talking and joking with everyone about how bad our football team was. Things couldn't have been better.

Then somewhere above the din of the crowd, I heard someone call my name. I thought I was imagining things, but I heard it again, closer and louder. I looked up and froze. There was my mom, standing in the middle of the crowd in pink house slippers and a long green T-shirt that hung down to her knees. She was holding her keys in one hand, so they jingled as she walked. She looked like a crazy homeless person.

I jumped out of my seat and strode quickly over to her. I could feel heads around me turning to stare. My friends called out to me, but I didn't have time to explain. I grabbed her arm and escorted her to the front of the restaurant as people gawked at the scene.

"Do you know what time it is?" she scolded. "I waited for you! Why didn't you call me?" Her voice was loud even above the noise of the crowd. I glimpsed the clock on the wall in the lobby; it was way past 11. It was my fault I had completely forgotten, but why did she have to come get me dressed like that? Why couldn't she just loosen up and let me have my fun?

The front section of the restaurant was pretty big, but I felt like the walls were shrinking in on me. She was invading my territory.

"We're leaving," she said firmly. I protested. I didn't want to leave like this. I was having fun. It was all so innocent, but my mom thought otherwise. In her eyes, this was a restaurant filled with large American jocks, not friends of mine. Just plenty of boys. But I knew once Mom put her foot down, there was no arguing.

"I'll meet you at the car," I said. Surrendering, I moped back to the table, threw down a 10 dollar bill, and left. My friends looked concerned. My mom and I fought the whole way home.

At school, everyone I knew asked me what happened, and why I left so abruptly. They asked if that lady was my mom, and I begrudgingly admitted that she was. I realized that no matter what I did, I would never feel like a normal teenager. My history, my family, would follow me like a shadow wherever I went. On television, they'd always show someone sneaking out of the house to go to a party or something. Out they'd climb from their window, down a tree, and into the car of their best friend, who would inevitably be waiting down the road and ready to party. I didn't have friends like that. I didn't know anyone with a car. I couldn't get out even if I tried; I felt like I was constantly being punished and kept in a prison. The more frustrated I got with her tight reign, the more my mom and I argued. I kept seeing reasons why I should be with my dad instead. If I wanted to buy something, I'd think, If only I lived with dad, *he'd* buy it for me. If I wanted to go somewhere that my mom wouldn't allow me to go, I'd think, *Dad* would've let me. Every argument with my mom just added fire to my burning desire to see my dad. It seemed he would know how to fix everything.

· ·

A lot of my time at home went to playing the piano. My piano teacher, Mrs. Audino, was a cranky woman in her fifties who yelled a lot and clearly didn't like children, especially my brother. She stuck mostly with a repertoire of classical music, making us memorize a song at a time and practice scales. Even though I loved playing the piano, I hated taking lessons from her because of her cantankerous attitude. My brother, who hated the piano and never practiced, had it worse—she would call him a loser and tell him that he would never amount to anything; he was just wasting her time. I felt sorry for him—I could be as mean as I wanted to John, but that didn't mean other people could. After my mom realized that she was just wasting her money, John was allowed to quit, while I, on the other hand, had to take piano lessons all the way until I graduated high school.

Despite those horrible times with Mrs. Audino, my love for music was stronger than ever. Peace and tranquility washed over me when I played the piano. It was comforting. I knew, though, that I was outgrowing classical music. In band, we learned to play contemporary music, so going home and playing classical pieces by Mozart or Bach felt so ancient to me, almost clunky. I begged my mom to get me the keyboard that I wanted. She was reluctant. It was so expensive. But she realized it would keep me busy at home.

One day, I came home from school and found a big box, all wrapped up, on my bed. I tore open the box and gently lifted out the keyboard! My mom had realized it would keep me busy at home, so she'd finally caved. I couldn't wait to try it out. It came with all these different beats and samples—more than 630 different sounds. There were thunder roars, claps, entire choirs, different combinations of beats and rhythms, and all kinds of other sounds. I used to get really

I couldn't wait to come home and try out new melodies and beats. In band, I learned to listen to music in layers. Listening closely, I would hear percussion, then on top of that I could make out the strings, and on top of that, a layer of woodwinds. In class, I would close my eyes and put those pieces together the way I wanted and create my own song. At home, I took songs we sang in church and restructured them on my keyboard to make it hipper and more contemporary. I'd find a drumbeat I liked, then add the melody and musical flourishes like flutes or marimbas on top of it. The keyboard unleashed that creativity I had in such abundance when I was that fearless little girl in Charlotte, gleefully singing my ABCs in front of that crowd at the international festival. It was like rediscovering a whole world that had been sleeping within me for years.

• •

Looking back now, I understand why my mom was so strict and overprotective. Traditional wisdom tells you that the man of the house provides safety and security for you and your family. You don't have to worry about strange boys coming around and trying to corrupt your daughter. Dad will be there to guard the door and protect the family. Without someone like that at home, my mom didn't have a safety net. My future, my brother's future, rested on her shoulders, but she couldn't be around all the time to guide us on the right path. I now understand how hard it must have been for her running a business by herself and raising two kids, and I'm thankful, even lucky. If my mom had been more flexible, I probably would have gone out more, especially given my social nature, and may have gotten myself into all kinds of trouble. Maybe I would have ended up pregnant and alone, just another teen statistic—my mom's worst fear.

Music can be a solitary thing. You don't really need anyone around to play. When you have a keyboard that provides all the different sounds you could ever want, why would you need someone else there? Everything you could want is right in front of you. Without that keyboard, I would not have had something constant there to keep me home and reveal my true love.

The keyboard really opened my mind to a different world, one where seemingly unreachable dreams were suddenly possible. Living in New Castle was like being trapped in a house with no windows or doors. There's just darkness all around you. In that kind of world, you tend to believe without question what other people tell you: you're worthless, you're ugly, or you have no future. You don't know any better, and you don't have any other kind of experience that can tell you differently. For me, that keyboard showed me there was another way. When I pressed all the different keys and buttons, I heard sounds I'd never heard before and I created pieces of music that were completely my own. It was like someone opened a hole in the wall and in a flash, blue light came flooding in. The keyboard was my escape from reality. All of a sudden I realized things didn't have to be the way they were. I didn't have to be that poor Asian girl who didn't have any money, who wore second-hand clothes, who came from a broken home. It became clear to me that I had a purpose in life, though I wasn't sure exactly what that was. But for once, I had hope. I knew I could be so much more. *Life* as I knew it could be so much more.

Chapter 3:

Free at Last

After I got my keyboard and gave in to my mom's strict demands, life seemed to get a little easier. The constant arguing lessened. Every day, I went to school. Then I came straight home and hit the books. Mom spent her time drilling into me the importance of getting an education and a professional job, and then finding a successful man to marry and start a family.

My weekends were spent volunteering at the Jameson Memorial Hospital as a candy striper. My mom wanted to expose me to the healthcare field in hopes that I would become a doctor like my uncle. I started in the x-ray department my freshman year, moving the following year to the dietary department, where I helped prepare and deliver food to the patients. My next year was spent working on the nursing floor units, where I interacted with patients directly. Most of the patients were very old, miserable, and lonely. It was sad to see them like that week after week. I wondered, "Where's their family?" I couldn't help but think about my dad and how lonely and miserable he must be without his kids.

Karen volunteering

My senior year I worked in the health administration office. That's where I met the CEO of the hospital, Thomas White. He had an office that was bigger than my living room, filled with cherry wood furnishings, plush oriental rugs, and fancy oil paintings. It seemed that all he did was attend lunch meetings and play golf. Working there gave me a glimpse of another kind of life that I was totally intrigued by. I wanted to know how I could become a CEO. Luckily, Thomas was approachable, and he suggested I get my bachelor's degree in finance and then a master's degree in health administration.

Karen's high school graduation

It became clear to me that college was my ticket out of New Castle. I studied hard, got good grades, and targeted New York University as my dream school. Its location in New York City, one of the top cities worldwide for finance, was ideal. Plus New York City was exciting for a small-town girl like me. All it took for me was one visit, and I could see myself getting swept up in the excitement of it all. The yellow taxis whizzing by, the noisy swell of traffic, the different kinds of people of every color and type rushing around you on the sidewalks. It was the complete opposite of everything I knew and hated about New Castle. But NYU was expensive. It cost about $30,000 a year to attend—money my mom and I simply did not have. Being the businesswoman that she is, my mom also reminded me that attending NYU was not a good investment. She argued that I would get distracted by the big city's fast-paced lifestyle and would end up partying and throwing away her hard-earned money. She wanted me to stay close to home and attend an in-state school because it was cheaper. She even resorted to having my pastor talk to me to try to convince me to stay near my family. I loved the hustle and bustle of New York, but inside, I knew they were right. I gave in and applied to Penn State, just about a two-hour drive away from New Castle.

Even though it was close to home, Penn State was a world apart. Nearly half my high school went to Penn State, but I never saw them. Thousands of kids descended on campus from all over the world. I decided to room together with my old friend Jennifer DiLorenzo for our first year. On move-in day, she and I found ourselves among thousands of other excited teenagers and nervous parents lugging suitcases from cars toward our dorm rooms. The dorms at Penn State were set up in different towers, each named after their location on the sprawling campus: East, West, Center, North, and South.

Jennifer and I were assigned to the East Towers, along with all the other freshmen. As we walked down the hall toward our room, I peeked into rooms with their doors propped open, getting a glimpse of kids setting up their dorm rooms, making friends, playing music. I couldn't help but notice that everyone was predominantly white. After we found our room, Jennifer easily made friends with the girls down the hall. They began chattering excitedly about the cute boys they had seen so far, and I soon found myself reverting back to New Castle mode. I couldn't really agree that I'd seen any cute boys on campus or around the dorms. They went on to talk about make-up and what cute clothes they all had. My awkwardness intensified. I didn't wear make-up. What was I going to talk about? My hand-me-downs or the stuff I stole years ago? I clammed up and concentrated on unpacking.

Welcoming Day on campus was like a carnival, complete with caricature portrait artists and "psychics" who would predict your future at Penn State and beyond. It was exhilarating to be walking among the crowds of new and different people, seeing the sights of campus, and getting a glimpse of what awaited us over the next four years of college. Colorful decorations hung from the buildings, and big welcome signs loomed overhead. Jennifer and I thought it would be fun to see what our futures held, so we headed over to the tarot card readers. I sat down at the table and the reader told me to choose four cards from the pile. Cautiously, I drew out four tattered-looking tarot cards. When she flipped them over, they all turned out to be knights. I had no idea what that meant.

"Wow," the reader said, looking up at me in surprise. "Looks like you're going to have plenty of men after you." I laughed. That sounded so ridiculous to me. Always the odd girl out in social settings, I just couldn't see boys in my future at all. They were the last thing on my mind.

Later, as I was walking back to the dorms, I heard someone call out, "Karen!" I was surprised—it seemed impossible that I knew anyone among the crowd of thousands of strangers. For a second I had a flashback to my mom, coming back to get me just like that night at Perkin's, but I quickly realized the voice was a male one. I turned and saw an Asian guy with a familiar face.

"Joe! What are you doing here?"

I was thrilled. Every summer back in high school, we used to go on these Korean church retreats, where Korean kids from nearby states would join us. That's where I met Joe Han. Joe couldn't have come from a more different background than me, but we got along great. Joe came from a wealthy family in Cincinnati, Ohio. His parents owned several businesses, so money was never an issue for him. In college, instead of doing laundry, he just bought new clothes. But he wasn't at all stuck up about it, he was actually very cool and very sweet. I was surprised to see him at Penn State, but also very happy to see someone I knew and got along with.

Joe invited me to come out to dinner with him and a few of his friends later that evening. They all turned out to be from his dorm building—and every single one of them was Asian. Eddie

Chao was Chinese, the quiet type. He was a little on the short side and, like Joe, came from a wealthy family. David was also Chinese, but seemed the opposite of Joe; he was tall and athletic, and actually pretty good-looking. His family wasn't that wealthy, but they did alright. Carlos was Filipino and grew up in Las Vegas. His family was pretty well off, too. They had all bumped into each other earlier that day and had instantly hit it off. I could see why. They were all so funny. They talked about random things and cracked each other up. Everyone was so easygoing. That first night having dinner with the boys was so much fun. I didn't feel any pressure to show how much I knew about the latest trends or clothing. I didn't feel like I had to prove something. Instead, I was relaxed and comfortable, more so than I'd ever felt in any social setting before. For once, I didn't have to worry about being able to relate about cute boys, clothes, or make-up. All I had to do was enjoy being myself. What a concept, I thought.

• •

Penn State was a huge school. There were something like 40,000 undergraduates and 30,000 grad students—the large majority of them white. Asians only made up about 2 percent of the total. But because there were so few of us, we all gravitated toward each other. It wasn't just Joe and his friends. Walking around campus, going to class or the library, random friendly Asian kids would come up to me and say hi. That first night in the dorms, I'd realized that I was the only person of color in a sea of white faces. Immediately I felt like I was back in high school all over again, only 24/7; I could feel myself shrinking back into the quiet, uncomfortable girl who never belonged and always felt left out. When I saw Joe and met his friends, it was like someone swept open these big, heavy doors to reveal a warm, wide world of other people who looked like me and thought like me. They took me out of that solitary existence that I had grown so accustomed to throughout high school. I didn't feel like I had to explain myself to pretend that I was someone who I wasn't. As Joe and his friends and I were laughing over dinner and joking about the dorm food, I thought, wow. They're including me. I'm hanging out with them. I realized that we were all equal. No one knew or cared about who we were in high school or how much money our parents had. It didn't matter. We were all here, at ground zero, to pursue a better future.

The five of us quickly became inseparable. Because we were all business majors, we had the same classes and the same daily schedule. People even called us "The Fab Five." We ate every meal together, went to class together, then hung out later, studying or visiting and meeting other kids. We went out every night, meeting new people. For the first time in my life, I called the shots on when I came home, or if I wanted to come home at all. Mom wasn't there to enforce her rules on me anymore. Sure, college freshmen all over the country probably felt the same way, enjoying their newfound independence for the first time without the watchful eyes of their parents. But for me, it felt different. That freedom meant more. I finally could come out of this shell that I'd been living in for so long.

There were other boys, too—particularly Jeff Lee. Jeff was my first real boyfriend. Aside from my disastrous foray into dating Jake in high school, boys remained a complete enigma to me. But I was feeling a little high from my newfound independence and so when Jeff started paying attention to me, I ran with it. Jeff was a sophomore, a Korean American who grew up going to American schools in Korea, so he was fully Americanized. All the girls thought he was hot. Yes, he was athletic and 6' 1", tall for an Asian guy, but I never lusted after him like the rest of the girls—I thought he was average. I did like him because we both played volleyball. I was a setter on my high school volleyball team, and Jeff had been the captain of his school's volleyball team. Maybe he was first drawn to me because I actually knew what I was doing on the court, unlike most of the other girls on my team. We ended up talking a lot, and pretty soon, we were studying together and hanging out outside of volleyball. I thought it was innocent at first, but when my Fab Five friends started to tease me about Jeff having a crush on me, I wasn't so sure. Every time I mentioned it to the other girls, they just brushed it off, saying, "Oh, he's like that with all the girls." I wasn't so special, they seemed to be really saying. But one day, he showed up at my dorm with a huge bouquet of flowers and a heart-shaped box of chocolates. He asked me to be his girlfriend. I said yes without hesitation. And those girls soon learned that they were wrong.

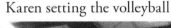

Karen setting the volleyball

My relationship with Jeff came and went. There were others, and they all ended up the same way. At first I'd be excited, but the boys wouldn't respect my Christian values and I'd feel smothered. Having a boyfriend was like having another version of my mom, and I didn't like having someone constantly asking me what I was doing or where I was going. Boys were difficult and I just didn't know enough about them to have a successful relationship. I guess I was young and experimenting. I figured if I went out with different guys, I would eventually know what I wanted in a man. I definitely didn't want to limit myself. I dated so many guys so quickly that one night, I ran into five of them at the same party! My friends teased me about it, but I just didn't want to settle for something or somebody that didn't make me completely happy.

Karen & best friend Grace Shin

The one person who understood where I was coming

from was my new friend, Grace Shin. Grace was the loudest Korean girl I'd ever met. She just didn't care what anyone thought of her. She would spout off the first thing that came into her mind, and usually it was something hilarious. One afternoon, I was sitting there watching a pickup basketball game after church and I heard a very loud voice behind me, yelling and laughing. I turned and saw Grace sitting by herself, just having a grand old time amusing herself with her own funny comments. We both started yelling out things at our friends on the court and cracking each other up. It wasn't long before we became inseparable. Unlike the Asian guy friends I had, Grace was just like me. She was a tomboy and loved sports. She didn't wear dresses or skirts or anything girly. Between her and my guy friends, I felt that we were carving out our own little world, and that big white world was just something I passed in the hallways on my way to other, more colorful places.

• •

Before my time at Penn State, I wanted so badly to fit in to that big white world I lived in, where I was constantly at odds with everyone else. I dyed my hair so that it was lighter. I wore all different types of colored contacts to change the color of my eyes. But no matter what I did, I was never one of them; I could never be white.

Grace and all the other Asian kids at college really changed my life. Through them, I saw that there was a much bigger world out there and that I could be embraced by it. I had never been around so many people who were my age and looked like me. Feeling comfortable and accepted, suddenly my Korean heritage seemed like an open book that was just begging to be explored by me.

For the first time, I wanted to know what it meant to be Korean, and I even started to feel a little bit of pride at being Asian. I joined different Asian student groups like the Korean Undergraduate Student Association. I also volunteered to teach little kids the Korean fan dance—the same one that my mom wowed the community with at the international fair so many years ago. I remember gazing up at her with so much respect when I was little, and now I felt proud that I was owning that part of my culture myself. Yes, I am Korean, I seemed to be saying with every movement of the fan. And yes, I am proud, I taught the kids. So in my sophomore year, when my dad offered to take me and my brother to Korea for the summer language program at Yonsei University, I jumped at the chance to visit my homeland for the first time.

Chapter 4:
Motherland

Brother John, Becky Yoon and Karen in Korea

Miraculously, my mom didn't try to prevent us from going. After all, the classes from Yonsei would transfer as school credits to PSU saving tuition money. Soon, we were cruising through the air, thousands of miles above the ocean on a red eye flight. Next to me, my brother John slept soundly, breathing in and out peacefully. With us was my college friend Becky Yoon, who was also going to attend the Yonsei program. We had a long, 17-hour flight ahead of us, and most of the passengers were asleep or watching movies—but I could barely shut my eyes. I had never been outside of the country before, but on top of that, I'd also never faced the prospect of spending so much time with my dad after all these years. I was really excited to see how he was. What did he look like now? What kind of life did he lead? I had no idea what to expect, but the excitement fluttered like butterflies in the pit of my stomach. I couldn't wait.

Yonsei is one of South Korea's top universities, and every summer, it hosts dozens of college students from all over the world who want to take classes to learn the Korean language, culture, and history. Among Korean American students, though, the program became known as party central for underage kids in a foreign country where the rules are much more lax than they are at home. Although I did my fair share of partying, there was no denying the cultural lessons the program taught me about my homeland.

When our plane finally landed in Korea, the sky was dark and it was nighttime. I looked out the window as we taxied down the runway and saw thousands of lights twinkling against the landscape. Coming in closer to Kimpo International Airport, I started to make out signs, large billboards with Korean characters written all over them. It was totally surreal. The only Korean sign I'd ever seen was for the Seoul Gardens Restaurant, the only Korean restaurant near campus. Here, every sign had Korean characters all over them. When we finally got off the plane after that exhaustingly long journey, Becky, my brother and I stretched our cramped legs and made our way to the baggage claim. Out of nowhere, a small kid, about six years old, randomly ran up to my brother and grabbed onto his leg. My brother and I looked at each other in confusion.

"Sorry, we don't have any money," John said, looking around uncomfortably. Then, we heard a familiar voice faintly yell, "Sam! Sam!" I turned and saw my dad. He was standing there with a woman standing beside him. The little boy turned around and ran back to him. My dad came over to hug us, then turned to the little boy.

"This is my son, Sam," he said. The little boy looked up at us. My brother and I were stunned. My dad had never mentioned a son in any of his correspondence all through the years. I didn't know what to say. I was shocked to find I have a half-brother. Then my dad introduced us to his wife. Double-shocker. He never mentioned her either. This entire time I'd imagined him as poor, lonely, and bored like myself. She bowed and spoke in Korean. I could see that she was a woman who cared about her looks. Her hair was carefully done and she wore make-up. A tight smile was drawn across her face. She didn't seem all too pleased to see us.

After we retrieved our bags from the baggage claim, we followed my dad and his new family out to the curb and piled into his jeep. We were all hungry, so we decided to stop at a restaurant before heading to my dad's house. My dad, a food-lover, didn't think twice about driving an hour out of the way to eat a good meal. Along the way, he tried to make small talk, catching up as best he could with his limited English and us with our limited Korean. He asked about my mom. We said she was doing fine. He told us that his son Sam was learning English in school, and maybe we could help him practice. He told us that he'd gotten into the import-export business. His new wife was just a housewife—a typical, submissive Korean lady, in my mind. She hardly said anything the entire time. I think it was partly because she didn't speak any English, but my dad could have translated somewhat for us. I could tell she felt kind of weird, and looking back now, I guess I couldn't really blame her. She was just a typical married woman with a family, but she was put in this awkward situation of playing host to her husband's estranged children from another marriage.

The restaurant was big and noisy. We sat in a large booth and soon several small plates of food arrived, nearly covering the table. I learned later these were called ban-chan, and were usually served before every meal. There were so many colorful dishes of all varieties: pickled spinach, marinated bean sprouts, scallion pancakes, salty-sweet fish cakes and, of course, spicy kimchi with big flecks of red chili, plus spicy hot fish soup and garlicky grilled meats. I took it all in—the sights and the smells, the sounds of Korean being spoken by everyone around us. While my dad lectured us about the huge bugs in Korea, John and I happily wolfed down all this delicious food. By the time we drove to my dad's house, we were drowsy, happy, and exhausted from all the travelling and eating. But as soon we pulled in to the driveway, I woke up.

Ban-chan – Photography by Brian Johnson & Dane Kantner

Driving up, I saw a huge complex rising before me. My dad lived in a luxury high-rise condominium. We knew he had gotten into the import-export business dealing in electronics, but we had no idea how well he was actually doing. He had three cars—something that only the really rich had in Korea. Outside each high-rise was a large soccer field lit up with bright lights, where older men came out every morning at 6 o'clock to hoof around with a soccer ball. My dad never mentioned that he was living in the lap of luxury.

Inside, my dad's condominium was small but nicely furnished. I felt exhausted and drained from the long trip, so I decided to take a shower before bed. The bathroom was completely different from what I was used to in America. There was no shower curtain or door, and the showerhead was built about midway up the wall instead of at the top like in America. I had to shower sitting down, with my rear end on the cold tile. The whole experience was really strange and new. When I got out of the bathroom, I saw that my dad's wife had set up our beds with Korean-style blankets and pillows, the small flat hard ones. Even though they were nothing like my comfy bed back home in Pennsylvania, the moment my head hit that pillow, I was out like a light and I slept heavily.

At 6 o'clock the next morning, my dad woke us up for breakfast. It was an unheard-of hour to get up in the morning, especially after all the traveling we had been doing. John and I begrudgingly got out of bed and groggily walked into the kitchen to find a huge spread of food laid out on the table like an elaborate feast. My dad's wife had woken up even earlier to prepare our breakfast, and she had gone all out, even baking fresh bread. It was one of the best meals I'd ever had. If nothing else, the woman could cook—I had to give her that. Afterwards, my brother and I went straight back to bed, full and content.

We stayed with my dad for a few days before our program started at Yonsei. During those days, my dad didn't say much. Even when he took us out to see the beautiful sights of Korea, it was still awkward to be around him. A few nights before we left to start the Yonsei program, he drove us more than an hour to another restaurant. This one was high up in the mountains. After we parked, we had to hike up a trail until we saw some lights and a restaurant built into the side of the mountain. It was as if we'd stumbled upon some secret, exclusive gem of a restaurant. Both John and I were impressed. Inside, we were led through the main section of the restaurant, where diners sat at tables and chairs that were carved from rock. I sat down on the stone chair, which was surprisingly comfortable, and realized that my feet were dangling over a small, gurgling stream. I'd never seen anything like it in America. Even in that stunning setting, we just made small talk. Dad was still as stern and serious as I had always remembered him years ago.

The evening before John and I began our program, Dad took us on a tour of the subway. He instructed us on how to get around town and doled out some money to each of us. It was our allowance, he said, that would cover basic necessities like food and transportation while we were living at the Yonsei dorms during the week. On the weekends, we were to come home. He told us all this in his serious, instructional way. The allowance he gave us was more than what we needed to get around, but my brother didn't agree.

One weekend during the program, John and I returned to my dad's apartment for the weekend, and I was in my room when I heard loud angry voices coming from the living room. I came out and saw my brother and my dad shouting at each other in front of Sam and his mother. My brother had asked for more allowance money to get around, and my dad, being the careful budgeter that he was, refused, saying John should have budgeted better. I knew my brother was spending his allowance on stuff he shouldn't have like partying, booze, and cigarettes, but I didn't say anything. Angrily, John started bringing up a lot more than just his allowance.

"You owe us a lot more than that!" he yelled at my dad. All these years while we were struggling to make ends meet with my mom, my dad was living in a luxurious condo. He had three cars and was making lots of money, and yet he never sent us any, my brother accused him. My dad's face went bright red and his face contorted with fury. I'd never seen either one of them so angry. I always thought of my dad as being slightly intimidating, but I'd never seen him act out or be confronted like that by anyone. He and my brother went at it.

I didn't think it was right for John to say something like that to my dad. I remembered all those times my dad had sent us things, and my mom would just tear everything up and throw it all away. She never wanted to have anything to do with him. For all I knew, maybe he *had* sent us money, but knowing my mom, she probably arranged with the post office to return any packages mailed from Korea. Finally, I tried to calm them both down by telling John I'd give him more money if he needed it. He begrudgingly backed down, but I could see that he was angry about more than just the allowance. After John's Yonsei program ended, he was supposed to return to my dad's house and stay with him. But he was too angry to go back, so he stayed with me, crashing on couches in the dorm building's lobby until my program ended. In return for the extra money I gave him, he wrote all my papers. I tried to put the argument out of my mind.

• •

It didn't take long for me to realize that all the Asian friends I had made at Penn State were just an introduction to the different world I was about to experience. All these people I was meeting and things I was learning about myself and my culture would come into play later on in my life in major ways. At Yonsei, I was surrounded by Korean American kids from all over the country, even as far away as California. I made friends with a few guys who went to the University of California, Los Angeles and Irvine. Unbeknownst to me at the time, I would bump into them years later when I moved out to L.A. While my dorm at Penn State was filled with white students, my dorm at Yonsei was the exact opposite. I found myself in a sea of kids just like me. My roommate was a girl named Sora. She was a tall music major from Chicago with long black hair. She was super talented at piano and pretty, and she knew it. We got along just fine, but she had a boyfriend back in the States, so she didn't go out too much with the rest of us. My main partner in crime was Claire, a Jersey girl who was totally wild despite her conservative style of dress. She often got mistaken for being Japanese because of her pale complexion, but she was Korean through and through, with a mischievous look on her face that just said, "watch out." She was up for anything—the perfect companion to experience all of Seoul's nightlife.

Claire and Karen

It was 1998 and Korean entertainment was just starting to blow up. Musical groups like H.O.T. and S.E.S. were at the height of their popularity in Korea. I even heard Korean pop songs being played by my Korean friends at Penn State. Claire and I went out almost every night. Those first few days, I still felt a little out of place when I walked around Seoul. A lot of people mistook me for being Chinese or Thai, probably because of the way I dressed—I guess my tomboyish clothes didn't help. I soon tired of people thinking I wasn't Korean, so I started doing my hair like the "gah-soos"—Korean pop singers. I put my hair up in funky styles and even started wearing dresses. I combed through all the Korean fashion magazines to get style ideas and tried to copy what I saw. Pretty soon, people stopped thinking I was anything other than Korean. But the one thing that gave my American roots away? My Korean was terrible. Luckily, Claire was fluent and was able to communicate for the both of us. With her looks, charm, and fluency in Korean, she got us in everywhere.

Clubbing in Korea was an eye-opening experience. I was only 19 years old and had never been clubbing before in the States so I had nothing to compare it to and no idea what to expect. With the legal drinking age of 18 years in Korea, clubbing seemed a rite of passage for youth, so virtually every night after class, Claire and I would go out. We avoided touristy areas like Itaewon and hung out where the locals—the real Koreans—went. We spent most of our time in the trendy neighborhoods of Apkujongdong and Kangnam, where all the fun was. Our first night at a popular club called Julianna's, we ended up hanging out with the owner, who "serviced" everything. That basically meant we got everything for free—all our drinks and food. And since we were girls, we also got in for free without paying a cover. The owner enjoyed our company so much he asked us if we wanted to go to his friend's club, Basia, and when we agreed, he drove us over in his Mercedes. I hadn't ever been inside a Mercedes, let alone known anyone who owned one. When we got there, we were treated like V.I.P.'s—more free drinks, more free food. Whatever we wanted, we got. It was amazing.

The club scene also introduced me to the concept of "booking," the Korean answer to meeting people at clubs. My first experience with booking was confusing. I was sitting in a club with my friends when the waiter came over and said something to me in Korean. Since my language skills weren't up to par, I looked at him, confused, and told him I didn't understand Korean. He kept repeating "booking, booking," to me. It seemed like he was trying to get me to go somewhere, so I gestured over to my friends. He said they could come, too. I didn't know what was going on, but we followed the waiter anyway as he led us over to another table full of guys who were drinking big bottles of whiskey. My friends told me that this was called booking—a cultural practice at Korean bars in which men would ask the waiter to bring over a particular girl they'd like to meet. Sometimes, the waiter would bring some cute girls over to the table of a big tipper without being asked. The waiter would get a big tip, the girls would get free drinks, and the guys didn't have to risk getting shot down. It was a clean, symbiotic relationship where everyone won. There were no expectations on the girls—our only obligation was to have a drink, chit chat, and maybe share a few laughs. We could leave whenever we wanted and go back to our table, open to be booked again by another group of guys.

Booking in Korea wasn't just an opportunity to get free drinks and food, though. Through booking, I also met some of Korea's top entertainers. It didn't take long for us to get to know the waiters at the popular clubs, so they always tried to book us to celebrity tables if any happened to be there. Once, I hung out with Woo-Suk Kang, the director of the Korean film "Two Cops," a blockbuster hit that is still talked about years later, even among Korean Americans in America. Another time, I met Raymond, one of the singers in the popular Korean pop group, Coyote. One look at Raymond and you could tell he was totally wild. He was very flirty and I knew to stay away from him, even as we partied, but it was fun. Of course, there was also the downside of booking. One night, the waiter brought me and my friends over to a wealthy businessman's table. They bought us a round of potanjoo, this Korean liquor that you pour into a shot glass, then drop into a glass of beer and down it all in one shot, just like a sake bomb. I don't normally drink, but that night, I had three. I was pretty much gone, and I lost all control of what I was doing or where I was. When I woke up the next morning back at our dorm feeling groggy and hung over, my friend Becky told me what had happened that night. The potanjoo had gone to my head, and the wealthy businessman tried to get physical with me. After she retold me the events of the previous night, bits and pieces of the night floated back to my mind. I vaguely remember her telling me, "Karen, this guy who's trying to hit on you is married and has kids. You need to get away from him!"

Despite meeting some slimy old men, the Korean social scene was full of opportunities, too. The country was just about to embark on what they called the "hall-yu," or the Korean wave. Korean pop music was being played on the radio all over Asia in Japan, Hong Kong, and China, Korean TV dramas were gaining popularity across the world, and stars like Rain were making a name for themselves. There were signs of the burgeoning entertainment business everywhere, even on the Yonsei campus. Camera crews would often ask us to act as background players in movies, videos, and shows they were shooting. I was even scouted by an agent who was looking for a Korean American female to be a VJ on a television show. I was very tempted to stay. But Mom said it was out of the question. If I stayed, I would have had to postpone the rest of college, and my education would've fallen by the wayside. Who knew if I would even have returned? Of course, my mom wanted me to finish school. "After you graduate, you can do whatever you want," she told me. "But for now, you need to come home." I turned down the agent, not realizing that my career in entertainment had yet to begin.

• •

Korea was a life-changing experience. I've never had so much fun in my entire life. There were crazy times with all my new Korean American friends, but what I remember too are the quieter moments. I was really glad to see my dad. Yes, it was awkward at times, but I felt like something I'd wanted all through my childhood was finally in my hands. I met relatives I didn't know I had—all of my dad's sisters, and several cousins too. I don't know who I met because of the language barrier and the Korean custom which has everyone calling each other "auntie" or "uncle," so it was confusing for me with my limited Korean to tell who I was actually related to. It didn't matter, though. I knew that would be the first and last time I would ever meet them anyway.

Father side of the family in Korea

Another part of the whole trip that really stuck a chord for me was learning all about Korean history. Part of the Yonsei program included a tour of the country, and as we traveled around, I was struck by how old Korea is. I knew that Korea had a long history, but it didn't really hit me until I saw all the ancient structures in person. I was awestruck at the tombs of ancient kings and was surprised by the tall, wide mounds of dirt and altars built next to the ocean. I couldn't believe that I was looking at the very same structures that my culture, my people, had built centuries ago. Together, the ancient crumbling buildings and the ocean seemed so timeless and permanent. Rice paddies stretched for miles, as far as the eye could see. I saw people, old men and women, somebody's grandparents, bending over and standing in lush, green rice paddies up to their knees. Their homes, little thatched structures, were held together by a hope and a prayer. These were real shacks, and they made me think about how lucky I was to be raised in America.

It felt strange to me. I felt this missing link tugging at my soul. A realization dawned upon me. I thought, I'm losing my language. I'm losing my cultural and ethnic identity. In Korea, all this became evident to me. Everything I saw on the tour of the country—all the people and the ancient structures, the food and the country—seemed so foreign to me, but somehow familiar at the same time. I felt disconnected, but I was trying very hard to relate.

Karen & friend exploring Korea

When we were standing at the departing gate at the airport, a distinct feeling of sadness washed over me. I didn't want to go. Plus, my brother was still angry at my dad, though my dad just tried to pretend nothing had happened. I hated that we were leaving on a bit of a down-note. For me, things were different. My world had permanently changed. My brother and I hugged our father goodbye, took one last look, and boarded the plane for the 17-hour trip back to America.

Back in America, all of my friends were happy to see me, but they teased me about my new Korean look. I wore dresses more often, I wore some make-up, and even wore my hair differently. Gone was the sports-loving tomboy and in her place was this new girl, trying to grow up and into my own skin. On the inside, I had changed as well. I now knew what it was that I wanted.

I wanted to embrace my culture, and I wanted to experience life to its fullest here in America too.

College opened up my world. It was those years at Penn State and in Korea that I felt freer than I'd ever been. I realize that teenagers everywhere go through similar experiences of feeling trapped by adolescence, poverty, or unpopularity. Being labeled a geek, a nerd, a loser—these are teenage experiences that can severely cripple your confidence and development. Moreover, being the poor Asian girl in my class and always feeling like I was on the outside looking in—in addition to the normal pains of being a teenager—truly took its toll on me. I had retreated so far into this shell that it seemed a long, long way before I could see the light telling me that there was a bigger world outside. Going to a bigger school, and more importantly, going to Korea opened my eyes. For the first time, I understand where I came from, and that released me from the painful years of my adolescence. It was a freedom that comes with confidence in knowing who you are. No one would ever be able to take that away from me.

Chapter 5:

We're Not in Kansas Anymore

Karen graduating Penn State

I was motivated more than ever to enter the real world so I sped through college, graduating in just three years. I learned much more than just the basics of finance. I learned there were other young Korean Americans just like me, and I discovered the roots of my culture in Korea. I unearthed a new version of myself, one that had been buried beneath all those layers of awkwardness, self-doubt, and exclusion built up over all those years. My graduation was a graduation in the truest sense; I really felt like I was moving on not just to my post-college life, but to an entirely new phase of me. I couldn't be more ready to take the next step, to experience what life held for me. I wanted to know what my future was—my *real* future—not something conjured up randomly by some card reader hired to entertain me.

My last year in college, I made money by working at the campus Dairy Queen. One day during my shift, a tall basketball player named Michael Rowlands walked through the door. Immediately, my heart skipped a beat. He was a senior who was "hapa," or half Korean and half white, and all the girls thought he was really cute, including me. I was a little flustered, so instead of saying anything, I handed him a free ice cream cone. He took it and smiled.

"I have hookups, too," he told me.

"Oh yeah?"

"At the movies. But you have to come with me."

Michael Rowlands & Karen Beck

We began dating shortly after that. Michael wanted to go to law school after college, so for spring break, we got on a plane and headed for Los Angeles to check out schools. As I gazed through the window on the plane, I saw how big Los Angeles was. There were miles and miles of tiny little houses, so many of them dotted with bright blue swimming pools. I imagined beautiful, blonde people lounging by them, sipping cold drinks, without a care in the world. Long, wide streets were lined with swaying palm trees. My eyes grew big—I had never seen a real palm tree before. I pushed through the crowd after we landed at LAX, and we stepped outside into the sunshine. The sun felt warm on my face and cast a golden light on everything around me—the airport, the palm trees, the hills in the background. All around me, the sound of cars honking was like music to my ears.

We soon found our way to Koreatown, where we'd be staying for a week with Michael's friend Tom. Koreatown was just a short half-hour drive northeast of LAX, but it might as well have been Korea itself. I felt the memories flooding back from my summer at Yonsei. There were Koreans everywhere—walking the streets, working in stores, eating at restaurants, driving around. They were store owners and office workers, and there were plenty of young Korean Americans hanging out, too. The sounds of Korean being spoken everywhere floated through the air wherever we were, from the gritty street to restaurants, and everywhere I looked there were signs with Korean characters. I felt right at home—maybe even more so than when I was in Korea. After all, I was the embodiment of Koreatown itself—one foot in America and the other in Korea. Half and half, and all jumbled up together. Hamburgers with a side of kimchi.

The location couldn't have been more perfect, too. The beach was just a few minutes' drive away, all the amazing restaurants of Koreatown were right at our feet, and Hollywood, with all its clubs, glittery star-marked streets, and touristy landmarks, was just to the north. It's true what they say about L.A. being the land of beautiful people. The people were hot and the food was great. There was nothing to dislike about it. I thought, maybe this wasn't a bad place for me to apply to a graduate school. I could get everything I loved about Korea—plus amazing weather and food—right here in California.

After graduation, I came out to L.A. again with Michael. He had decided on a law school in Orange County, a predominantly white, wealthy enclave about an hour south of Los Angeles. I had my sights set on graduate school at UCLA. But UCLA required all applicants to have at least two full years of real work experience. Plus, I had to live in L.A. at least one year to qualify for in-state tuition, which would've been the only way I could've afforded to go there.

I found an apartment in Westwood, a small community right on the outskirts of the UCLA campus. My new roommates were all very excited to meet me. They all rushed to the door and crowded around me when I arrived. They helped me bring my bags inside and started talking all at once. They had decided to give me a true "L.A. welcome," so that night we all went to a sushi restaurant for dinner. I never had sushi before and was excited to try something new. When we walked inside the tiny Japanese restaurant, I was immediately greeted by the briny scent of the ocean and fresh seafood. All the sushi chefs were dressed in white, some with tall chef's hats, and others with bandannas tied around their head. They yelled out a greeting to us in Japanese, and then sat us down at a large table. I was shocked to see that most of the people eating there were white, not Japanese. They were all downing the bite-size morsels of raw fish that the chefs were laying out before each guest. I decided to try sushi with an open mind. The pieces of fish were such pretty little things, and the whole ritual of mixing the spicy wasabi paste in the soy sauce, then dipping each piece before popping it in my mouth, was fun.

We had a blast getting to know each other that first night, and I hoped that my new roommates and I would become friends. Unfortunately, for the most part, they kept to themselves and had their own dramas: boys and bulimia. So, I did my own thing, which was fine. That also meant I had to put my relationship with Michael on hold. After all, I had to find a job, which didn't turn out to be so easy.

I worked a lot at Penn State. Aside from dispensing ice cream at Dairy Queen, I took several additional part-time jobs, including one working for the wardrobe department at the local concert hall. I was the girl who made sure Janet Jackson's costumes were properly laundered and packed away before the show ended. I saw a lot of concerts from backstage then. I also worked the overnight shift at the front desk of my dorm from 11 p.m. until 7 a.m., basically getting paid to do my homework. In between all my part-time jobs and my full-time class schedule, I was stretched thin, but I was able to save up a lot of money for my move to the West Coast. Still, I was determined to find a job as soon as possible once I got to L.A. I had earned my degree in finance early, so I figured my resume would make me in demand, and I would be able to command a high salary.

I started hitting the pavement that first week I got to L.A. It was June, and I was traveling around town in a heavy business suit, meeting with about three or four different companies a week. I didn't have a car yet, so I took taxis and buses everywhere. L.A.'s infamous heavy traffic burned a deep hole in my pocket. I'd spend hours waiting in the hot sun for the bus to arrive, and then I'd pile on in my suit and heels alongside homeless people and random strangers from who knows where. Back in New Castle, no one rode the bus. Everyone had a car, and the town was small enough that you could easily get around town. Penn State was easy too. We had the school shuttle system, so everyone was somehow related to the school. L.A., in comparison, was huge. I needed to save every penny, even if that meant I had to walk around all day long in the heat and take the bus.

Interviewing was just as tough. I'd gather myself together, praying for no traffic and trying not to sweat too much on my way there, and then I'd walk up to these huge buildings of glass and steel with fountains in the courtyard. The working world was so stately and intimidating. My nerves made me jittery and my palms were clammy, and the interviewer would look me up and down, as if judging whether I was worthy to work there. I got some offers, but the pay was so disappointingly low that I rejected them left and right. I couldn't understand why I was getting so low-balled. Finally, one of the interviewers told me flat out that I was asking for outrageous salaries. In L.A., starting yearly salaries for new graduates were in the $20,000 to $30,000 range. But I was asking for at least $40,000 thousand dollars a year, which was standard on the East Coast. I realized pretty soon that I was going to have a tough time getting a job with a salary in that range. It didn't help that I was also competing against people with a lot more experience who were also asking for that kind of salary. It was July, and the weather was heating up. I was constantly drenched in sweat, tired of searching, and feeling pretty discouraged watching all the money I saved slowly run out. My mom kept calling, leaving me messages about how worried she was about me. I hadn't phoned her in weeks, avoiding the eventual question she would ask: Have you found a job yet? I didn't dare tell her the truth. She was already wary of me coming out to L.A. in the first place. Here I was, a month into my new life out in the West Coast, and I was still jobless, barely paying the bills. I just didn't want her to worry and I refused to ask for help. I was on my own and wanted to figure things out for myself.

There was only $300 left in my bank account when I found out about headhunters. They sounded like weird cannibals, but it turned out they're professional job searchers who get paid a commission by companies looking to hire people like me. The minute I heard this, I signed up with AppleOne Employment Agency and also with some background casting agencies, which hired all kinds of regular people to be extras on film and television sets. I thought some background work would help tie me over until I found a real job; plus I figured it would be easy with all my theatre experience from high school. One agency in particular even specialized in Asian casting. I sent them my pictures, and soon got a job as an extra on a movie called "Dark Blue," with Kurt Russell and Scott Speedman. It was a forgettable movie. I played a cocktail waitress in a strip club. They gave me a skimpy outfit to wear and I walked around the set trying not to look as uncomfortable as I felt inside. In between filming, though, the lead actors actually talked to the extras, helping me feel less uncomfortable. As weird as I felt, my first real Hollywood experience was so much fun that I looked forward to the next job. A couple weeks later, I got a call for another job, this time on the set of a Japanese television commercial with Nicholas Cage for Sanyo Pacchinko. I played a television reporter. I got paid about a hundred bucks per day of shooting.

Karen with Kurt Russell

Karen with Scott Speedman
on set of Dark Blue

Even though it wasn't a lot of money, I was having a lot of fun working as an extra. It was easy work, and I loved being star-struck with all those celebrities like Nicholas Cage. I figured I could keep doing this, so I picked up a copy of LA Weekly to see if I could find any other acting jobs. I flipped to the back pages, where rows and rows of tiny ads were crammed together, advertising everything from theatre work to moving supplies. There, buried among all those ads, I saw a listing for escort services. What caught my eye was the pay: $500. The number practically jumped off the page. But what the hell was escort services? Was it possible to get paid just to escort people around? The ad said I could make *at least* $500 in one night. That was money I could really use, so I picked up the phone and scheduled an interview.

Looking back now, I was pretty gutsy and very, very naïve. I had no idea what I was setting myself up for, but I was so desperate for money that I was blinded to the dangers of L.A. Coming from a small town and a very sheltered life, I guess I didn't naturally have that suspicious radar in me. All I knew at the time was that my top priority was to find a job and succeed in L.A. I needed to prove to my mom that I could.

• •

It was a bright sunny afternoon in the middle of the week. I walked into a Starbucks and anxiously looked around. I didn't exactly know whom I was meeting, just some guy, a managerial type. I sat down and waited for a long time, scrutinizing the face of every male that walked in the coffee shop, before I finally felt someone tap me on my shoulder. I turned to face a tall, bleach-blonde man, about 40 years old, looking down at me.

"Karen?" he asked.

"Yes, that's me," I stammered.

He was wearing jeans, a Hawaiian shirt, and sandals. Both his ears were pierced, and when he spoke, he sounded like a surfer. I got the impression that he was an older man trying hard to look young and cool. He definitely didn't seem like a manager and I had my first pang of suspicion hit me. But I was there already, so I felt I might as well talk to him.

I followed him to a table in the corner and he pulled out a chair for me.

"Have you done escort work before?" he asked in a low voice, looking around.

"No, but I don't think it should be too difficult." Then I continued, "But then again, it probably is difficult, being that the pay is so high."

He smirked.

"It's not difficult at all, Karen. In fact, it's rather easy. All you have to do is just keep lonely men company and, if they ask for more, you charge for more…a lot more." He was in full sleaze-bag mode now.

"Well, what more would they want?" I was sincerely curious.

"Honey, it could be anything. How about I set you up with your first client? We'll go from there."

He was pushing me to accept even though I had no experience and clearly had no idea what he was talking about. I had a bad feeling in my gut. To bide my time, I told him I had to think about it and would call him back.

"Just try it out once and then make your decision. You can't say no without at least trying. I guarantee it's quick, easy money—especially for you. You're young, pretty, and Asian. If you dressed a little sexier, men would be willing to spend big dollars on you."

I wasn't sure what he meant. He was vague with his answers. I was so nervous my hands were shaking. I'd never heard of escort work before, so I had no idea it could be anything bad. I was open to trying out new things, especially in L.A., so I caved to his pressure and figured I'd see what it was all about.

"Okay," I said in a small, nervous voice that didn't sound like my own. I would meet my first client that Friday.

As I walked in the afternoon sun back to my apartment, a vague, uneasy feeling began to overtake me. The more I thought about this escort business, the more I freaked out. Would I be pressured into doing something I didn't want to do? Would the customers be sleazy? I felt dizzy and anxious, and suddenly felt very exhausted. I got home and curled up on my bed, unable to shake that feeling.

The rest of the week, I tried to operate as if everything were normal, but I just couldn't put Friday out of my mind. I didn't know what to expect. All I knew was that someone was coming to pick me up around 7 or 8 o'clock that night. I tried to ignore that nagging feeling until the day came. And it came pretty quickly.

It was Friday morning when the doorbell rang.

Feeling a little foggy, I opened the front door and my mouth fell open.

"Karen. I have a one-way ticket for you and me, back home."

My mom was standing there, clutching two plane tickets. Her eyes were brimming with desperation and worry.

I have to admit I was a little relieved to see her. But I was also mad. It was just like we were in Perkin's again, her showing up unannounced to interrupt this life I was trying to make for myself. We stood there in the front doorway, arguing. She insisted that I come with her. I refused. I yelled at her for wasting her money on such a bad idea. I was in L.A. to stay. Even if I made bad decisions and totally screwed things up for myself, I would be the one to pay the consequences, and I made that commitment when I came out. There was just no way that I was going home before I even gave myself the chance to fail.

I told my mom to come inside.

• •

My mom had spent so much of her adult life worrying over me and protecting me from everything that she was having a difficult time letting go. The entire time I was in L.A., she was worried sick. When she hadn't heard from me in weeks, she knew something was wrong. She scrounged up what money she had and flew out to "save" me. It's as if her mother's intuition gives her a psychic ability to know when I'm in trouble, or when I've done something she wouldn't approve of, wherever I am.

I've always believed that there is no such thing as a coincidence and that people were put on this earth for a reason. I'm sure plenty of other people have said this before, but I look back at times like this and I realize there have been some moments in my life when some twist of fate or luck turned things around for me, just when I was standing on the edge of a cliff. Many times, my mom's intuition had a lot to do with it. I remember many years ago, when I was only about five years old, standing in the kitchen of our home in Charlotte with the refrigerator door open. It was one of those painfully hot, sticky summer afternoons, and I was dying for something cold and sweet to drink. My mom was in the bathroom, taking a cool bath and having a quiet moment for herself. I grabbed a bottle of red juice and twisted open the cap. My little brother John started whining at me to share some with him. I yelled at him to be quiet and he started to cry. I wanted the juice all to myself. Eyeing him, I pounded it down. He started crying even louder and ran into the bathroom to get my mom.

"Mom, Karen's drinking juice and she won't give me any!" he yelled.

"What?" My mom froze. "We don't have juice!" She burst out of the bathroom in a towel and ran into the kitchen. I was lying on the floor, barely conscious. She carried me into the car and rushed me into the emergency room. I had drained a large bottle of children's liquid Tylenol. Doctors pumped my tiny stomach, and I came home, a very lucky girl.

• •

I admit it was comforting to know that my mom was right there. My circumstances didn't seem to dire, and it turned out she came at just the right time. The phone rang. It was the headhunter.

"You were expensive, but Panasonic wants you," she told me. I got the job! My mom whooped for joy, and I couldn't be happier. I blew off the escort service.

My mom spent the night. The next morning we quickly decided that I needed a car to get to my new job, so we visited several dealerships. At the end of the day, mom helped me pick out a black four-door Dodge Neon ES. It was $17,000 out the door and it came with power doors, steering, locks, and even a sunroof. I got in the driver's seat and felt the cool, smooth steering wheel beneath my grip. *This* was the feeling of success. I drove off the lot, the wind rushing through my hair. Next to me in the passenger seat, I looked at my mom, who was smiling. She didn't have to say anything. I knew she was happy.

That weekend I drove my mom around touristy spots in Los Angeles to get her acquainted with my new home. She was slowly letting me go and learning to accept my decisions, accept that I was turning into an adult. She left for New Castle shortly thereafter. I couldn't help but cry out for relief that I finally got a job.

Karen and her Mother at Universal Studios

Now it was time for me to find a new home, one where I'd start the new chapter of my life. I found an apartment in Burbank to be closer to my job. It was a tiny studio, which I shared with one other person—Gonzalo Gonzalez. Gonzalo was an actor-slash-waiter and bartended at a restaurant called Islands while he waited for his big break. There were no beds. He slept at one end of the room, and I at the other. We were there only three months before the walls really started to close in on us. It was just too small, but neither of us had enough money to get a bigger place unless we found other roommates. So we moved to a two-bedroom apartment in nearby Sherman Oaks. I shared my room with Dahlia, a pretty Nicaraguan girl from Berkeley who was interning at The Tonight Show with Jay Leno. Meanwhile, Gonzalo shared his room with Anna, a foreign student from Guatemala who was going to school at California State, Los Angeles. For just $300 a month each, we were finally making it happen, each of us taking our first tiny steps to pursue our dreams.

Roommate Gonzalo Gonzales

Life in the corporate world was definitely different. For one year, I followed the breakneck 9-to-5 routine. I got up early, I went to work, and I came home every night to my makeshift family—all my roommates. Bit by bit, I saved up enough money to pay rent and all my bills. Life seemed to be looking up. But just as I felt I was settling into my new life, everything changed.

Coincidentally, I knew a fellow Penn State alumnus named Stephen who worked in the IT department of Panasonic's headquarters in Secaucus, New Jersey. Stephen was friendly, so he warned me about what was coming: Panasonic was downsizing, and my job was in danger. The headquarters office was starting to lay off employees. People were losing their jobs. It wouldn't be long before the same happened at other Panasonic offices around the country, including mine.

Panasonic employees

I panicked. I was still one year short to apply to UCLA's graduate program. I turned instead to University of Southern California, or USC, which only required one year of work experience, but the tuition was exorbitantly high and there was only two months left before the deadline to attend the fall semester. I would have to take out a hefty $60,000 loan and dedicate a month to studying the GMAT. The thought of walking around in the summer heat in my dark business suit interviewing for jobs scared me, so I bit the bullet, took the GMAT, and applied to USC. For weeks, I waited nervously, wondering what my life was going to look like in just a year. Would I be unemployed and broke again? Or would I be a grad student? After what seemed like ages, I opened the mailbox and saw an envelope from USC. I opened it hastily.

"We are pleased to accept—" I felt a wave of relief wash over me. Just a few days before, Panasonic had begun to lay off people in my department. I got out just in the nick of time.

Chapter 6:

The Surreal World

When the new semester—my first as a graduate student—came around, I was filled with excitement. The life of a student felt carefree and fun compared to working my corporate job. Every day, I looked forward to walking around the beautiful Trojan campus, taking in the trees and squirrels instead of sitting at a desk underneath fluorescent office lighting. It was an almost idyllic existence. But the one thing about student life that I didn't love? Feeling broke again. I had a full course load and although I had some money thanks to a school loan, it all went toward books, groceries, and rent. I knew I was going to need a part-time job to supplement what little money I was getting in financial aid.

My roommate Gonzalo told me he makes $40,000 a year just waiting tables. I knew I couldn't make that much with a full-time school schedule, but I could work nights and weekends and make enough to be comfortable. I hit the pavement again, this time looking for a fun, stress-free, part-time job waiting tables. Since Sunset Boulevard seemed to be the hub of all the popular restaurants, I made my way down the street, stopping in at each eatery and filling out applications. Then I saw the "help wanted" sign outside the Laugh Factory. Sitting a little bit away from the main drag of Sunset Boulevard, the Laugh Factory was a famous comedy club that drew a sizeable crowd each week to see the stand-up comedy world's biggest stars. I stepped in from the summer heat and the noisy traffic outside to an interior that was dark, quiet, and cool. On the walls hung rows and rows of photos of every major comic I had ever heard of. Jerry Seinfeld, Rodney Dangerfield, Bob Sagat—there were dozens of photographs all over the club, all personally autographed, some with funny notes or drawings. It was like a museum chronicling every comedian that had ever graced the stage there. I walked in further and asked about the job posting out front. The manager told me I needed to turn in my resume and headshot. Apparently in Los Angeles, they really did take this actor-slash-waiter thing literally. I played along and turned in a photo of me with a resume and soon got a call, telling me they didn't have any openings for a server, but they needed a hostess. I accepted immediately.

Laugh Factory

Being a hostess was pretty easy, except for one part of my job—getting the crowd of people waiting on the sidewalk to form some sort of line before doors opened for the show. I had never had to lead a group before; I had always been in the background of things. It felt awkward trying to command dozens of strangers who couldn't care less what I was saying. Outside the club, I attempted to yell at the crowd to get them to line up, but the noise of all the heavy traffic on Sunset just drowned me out. I'd try to yell louder, but everyone would just ignore me. A few people might look my way, but then turn back to their conversations. Somehow, over time, I learned to herd them into a line and usher them inside the club on time. Some even slipped me $20 bills to get them up front.

DJ Eque and Karen

Between these little tips and my part-time wage, the Laugh Factory helped me pay my way through school. But more than that, it helped me find my true calling. I usually worked Tuesdays, Fridays, and Saturdays. But one week, I switched shifts with another hostess and ended up working on a Sunday night. It was a completely different world. Sunday nights at the Laugh Factory were called Chocolate Sundaes. The comics were mostly experienced performers from Black Entertainment Television (BET) and Comicview. The vibe was cool and completely different from every other night. The crowd was predominantly black, hip, plus they had music, thanks to a DJ. Every Sunday night, a DJ named DJ Eque would spin from the second floor. She had spun for hip-hop artists like Faith Evans and Uncle Luke. She was a black female DJ who could command the entire room by getting on the turntables, and I remember thinking that was just the hottest thing. She'd put on a song, and then I'd watch the crowd's reaction. The vibe in the whole room would change with each new tune. To someone who couldn't even get the attention of a handful of people outside a comedy club, her ability to pump up a crowd like that with her music was just amazing. I just *had* to talk to her, so I ran upstairs to the DJ booth. All my words were rushing out in a flurry; I was like an excited little kid. *This is so cool! How did you get started? Where did you get all this?* I bombarded her with questions. She was busy spinning, but she was nice enough to talk to me for a few minutes. She told me to go to the Guitar Center, a local music store, and they would help me out.

Chocolate Sundaes

The next time I had the chance, I rushed to the Guitar Center, which was down the street from the Laugh Factory. I found the pro-audio area and saw the turntables. My heart was pounding so hard it felt like it was going to fly out of my chest. My fingers ran over the switches and sliders on the mixer; then touched the round slip mats. I was completely entranced by the turntables as I moved the metal disc back and forth. Then I saw the price tag: $500...*per turntable*. I needed two. Plus $300 for a mixer, $200 for headphones, and another $200 for needles...not to mention records! All my money was tied up in student loans and I was barely making ends meet. It would have been absurd to blow six months worth of rent on DJ equipment. And for what? All I knew was that I hadn't felt this kind of excitement since I laid my eyes on the keyboard back in high school. It was such a gamble, but something about it just pulled at me. In my mind, I saw the crowd at the Laugh Factory, the expressions on their faces. With the first beats of the song, the DJ's music just seemed to transform them somehow. It wasn't just that people were having a good time. The music made them feel happy. With one song, they could be plunged back into good memories from a past time, and with another, they could be singing along to the latest hit at the top of their lungs. I admired how calm and cool DJ Eque looked up there with her headphones. My mind was at war.

Come on Karen, don't be stupid.

The feelings the turntables gave me were indescribable. They were like the ocean's waves, pulling me out to sea.

You can't afford to blow six months of rent on this. This is crazy!

I didn't have to say or do anything; I just let the waves take me. I was pulled toward the cash register, where I stopped and heard myself tell the cashier that I wanted to buy the turntables. I felt the blood drain from my face. I quickly went through the transaction and someone helped me load everything into my car. My heart was racing. I couldn't wait to open the boxes at home and touch the turntables, feel them beneath my fingertips, and examine the needles up close.

I got back to the apartment and tore into the boxes. My roommates rushed out to see what the commotion was all about. They were just as excited as I was. We sat around the living room, playing with all the little knobs and levers, the turntables and needles. I was so excited. Gonzalo was laughing. He couldn't believe I'd spent all that money on these turntables. But I didn't care what he thought.

For the next few days, I played around with the turntables, getting to know the equipment. I found out about a record store on Melrose called Fat Beats and went to check it out. That's where I bought my first record, the Beatnuts' "Watch Out Now." I bought two copies so I could practice on the turntables. In order to learn how to deejay, you have to learn how to mix first, meaning playing two records at the same time so that it produces just one sound. Timing is everything in deejaying. If one record is even slightly faster than the other, the result will be a train wreck of sound. So the art of mixing is to be able to get two songs at the same speed, which wasn't as easy as it sounded.

I found out that there was another record store closer to my house on Ventura called Groove Ryders. I walked there almost every day and asked the guys for tips. I remember going in one day and talking to the guys there like I was an excited kid in a candy store. "Hey, do you guys know how to scratch?" I inquired. Scratching meant creating various types of scratching sounds using one hand to move the record back and forth and the other to move the crossfader on the mixer. I tried to do it, but couldn't quite grasp the concept or get the coordination down yet. I spent hours learning how to work the turntables and master the artistry of it all. I broke so many needles and wore out a lot of records. It was difficult, but slowly, I was getting there.

After about a month of constant practicing, I mentioned to my boss at the Laugh Factory that I'd bought turntables and was teaching myself to deejay. He was really excited for me and immediately offered to let me spin at the club some nights. He suggested that I start out with Monday nights, also known as Latino Night. Monday night tended to be a little slower and easier to navigate, so it would be a good night to deejay in public for the first time. When Monday rolled around, I lugged in all my heavy equipment—40 pounds for each turntable, plus more for the mixer and my small crate of records. Then I set it all up and got ready to play for the Latino comics' crowd. I was nervous before I started, but it turned out to be easier than I expected. I would just pick a record, hit play, and then press stop when the comics were ready to perform. Once I got the hang of that, I even started testing out some of my scratching skills and would scratch a song in. The audience looked happy, and I was overjoyed.

Eventually, I became a regular fixture on Latino nights. I got to know my equipment really well, and it wasn't very long before I got really good at setting up and breaking down quickly, a skill that would come in handy later on. The comics started to take notice of my deejaying skills, and soon they were incorporating me into their routines. Monday night's host, Jeff Garcia, would sometimes tell a funny story about picking up women in clubs and he'd have me play a certain song to help illustrate the joke. Other comics would ask me to introduce them with certain songs they liked as they walked on stage, or add music at different points in their act, too. I came to enjoy being a part of the comics' stand-up routines. The music I added to their shows not only got the audience excited, but it also got the comics pumped up too. They'd feel more comfortable on stage and have more fun, and in turn, so would the audience and I.

· ·

The time I spent working at the Laugh Factory left a lasting impression on me. I think that discovering something I loved to do—something that I could share with others—helped me to break out of my shell a little more and opened up my world of experience. As I was going to school, working, and learning to deejay, I also enjoyed just being young and living in one of the biggest, most famous cities of the world. Los Angeles has so much to offer, especially in terms of its nightlife. It's especially exciting when you're young and living on the edge of Hollywood. I took full advantage of my circumstance and dove right into LA nightlife. It wasn't just fun and games, though. It was a learning experience. Going out to clubs also gave me a chance to see and hear real club deejaying up close.

I didn't go alone; fortunately I had two good friends by my side. There were plenty of servers and bartenders at the Laugh Factory, but I clicked with two more than any other: Tanya, who worked at the box office, and Noelle, another hostess. Together, the three of us had some great times at the clubs. It didn't hurt that both of them were smoking hot. They were total guy magnets. I'd never hung out with girls who got so much attention from men, and I was constantly amazed by how many guys my two friends would get.

Karen, Tanya Lemelle & Noelle Flores

We usually hit the clubs after work, staying on Sunset Boulevard along with all the other club crawlers. Who says no one walks in LA? On any given weekend night, Sunset Boulevard was practically a promenade of people walking up and down, checking each other out. Occasionally, you'd spot a celebrity or two. Our favorite clubs were Saddle Ranch, Dublin's, and Miyagi's. Most of the time, we hung out at Dublin's, a popular club on the Sunset Strip that looked like a worn-out Irish pub, just crawling with people. Sometimes it would be so crowded we'd have to push our way up the stairs to the table seating area. Tanya and Noelle would lead the charge, dozens of guys pawing after them, with me following behind. We were like a caravan of three, making our way through a dense forest of men.

Tanya likes to say we were "GHET-*TO*" back then. I was a broke college student and Tanya was a struggling actress, so between us, we didn't have a lot of money. We would pile together into one car to save on gas and parking and then get into clubs for free. Sometimes the clubs or house parties would have buffets, so we would have dinner there, and guys bought us drinks—we never bought our own drinks. It was easy, of course, since Tanya and Noelle got so much attention. I was always happy just being the quiet one, watching all the action from my little corner of the room. In fact, that's how I got my DJ name. Whenever we went out, I was always the one quietly observing from the sidelines. One night, a comic we were hanging out with named Reggie Blaze took notice. He pointed out that I never really had much to say because I was so shy, so he called me DJ SHY. I immediately related. It perfectly captured my personality and it stuck with me. Yes, I'm shy, but being shy gives you the chance to observe and take in everything around you without being noticed. That was important to me because I learned so much just from watching and listening to the world around me.

Comic Reggie Blaze & Karen Beck

Inside the clubs, while the girls flirted with their various suitors, I sat there listening to the music, taking note of what the DJ was doing and watching the crowds' reactions to his or her every move. I took mental notes on the songs they played and was constantly amazed at how powerful music was in setting the mood in a club. A good DJ could totally own the crowd and give them an unforgettable experience. In contrast, a bad DJ could just as easily turn a night into a dud. That kind of power mesmerized me.

Even though I didn't always actively participate in what was going on at the clubs, that's not to say I didn't get any attention at all. I was meeting all kinds of people then and going out a lot, so naturally I attracted some guys as well. One night working at the Laugh Factory, some guy tried to get my phone number, but I wasn't feeling it. Later, Tanya told me that the guy who was hitting on me was Richard Pryor's son, Wendell. But frankly, I wasn't really into dating outside my race at that time. Asian guys were still the ones that caught my eye. Tanya dated a lot of black men because she was more attracted to them than anyone else. She really opened my eyes to different races, other than just Asian and white. So when an aspiring black comic named Sammy Washington started flirting with me, I was intrigued.

Sammy was light-skinned and had beautiful green eyes. He used to play football for Portland State and was trying to make it as a comedian. He was very persistent, calling and emailing me all the time. I was interested, but I held back a bit because I was kind of unsure about him. He had this swagger and confidence, the kind that comes from lots of dating experience, and he was very mature—maybe that made me feel a little wary. But after months of trying to get me to go out with him, I finally gave in. On our first date, he brought me flowers, which totally caught me off guard—I mean, how many men still do that nowadays? We went to dinner and talked about everything. He asked me tons of questions about the kinds of guys I liked to date and what I expected in a relationship. I still wasn't sure about him. He wanted our second date to start off with a bang, so he took me to Vegas. I'd never been to Vegas before and I have to admit, I was a little scared. It's not called "Sin City" for nothing, and I'd always heard it was full of bad people and a ton of gambling. And here I was, going with a guy I barely knew. I didn't know if Sammy had any expectations or anything, so I tried to go with an open mind. We checked into the Hard Rock Café and headed for the pool. The hotel had just opened, so the pool was empty, except for a handful of people. It felt like we had the whole place to ourselves. We hung out, ate great food, and I relaxed a bit and ended up having a good time. Later that night, Sammy had the hotel sprinkle rose petals all over the room, but he didn't pressure me into anything. On the long car ride home through the desert, I realized I'd actually had a really nice time. I decided that I would like to be Sammy's girlfriend.

From the beginning of my deejaying career, Sammy was my cheerleader. He believed in me and really encouraged me to pursue it full force. He even taught me all about old school hip-hop music because I didn't know that much about the history of that genre. One night after I finished my shift, Sammy wanted to take me to a nightclub for a surprise. It was late and all the clubs were already closing, but luckily we got there just in time to catch Spinderella, the legendary DJ from Salt-N-Pepa, finishing her set and leaving the club.

Spinderella, Sammy Washington & Karen Beck

Thanks to him, I learned about earlier hip-hop groups like Kid 'N Play, so one night when Kid made a surprise appearance, I was glad that I knew who he was and happened to have one of his songs in my crate. After Kid 'N Play disbanded, Kid went on to try out a career in stand-up comedy. It wasn't unusual to get surprise big-name performers at the Laugh Factory, and they usually got preference over the lesser-known names who were scheduled to perform. The night that Kid showed up, I played their hit, "Rollin' with Kid 'N Play," as his closing song. When he finished his set, he looked up with a mixture of surprise and affection then gave me a huge smile and a wink.

Even though Sammy was a great supporter, he wasn't very honest about some other things. I soon found out he'd lied to me about a number of things, including his age and marital status.

Apparently, he had another girlfriend in Portland who was raising their baby. Once the truth came out, we didn't last long. The last time I saw him was at the Laugh Factory. I was there one night with a new date and a few friends. We saw each other from across the room, and that was the end of that.

After Sammy, I dated some more people I met at either the Laugh Factory or the clubs. Tanya started dating a pretty well-known rapper named Rass Kass after we'd met him one night in a club. I ended up dating his roommate, and through them we met some of their good friends, well-known West Coast music artists. Often, we would go to Exzibit's house in Northridge to have dinner. Rass invited us to hang out in Larrabee Studios where Dr. Dre would record beats. Will Smith would drop by to borrow studio time to record for his movie, *Independence Day*.

I also dated some actors, but in the midst of all that going out, I continued to focus on my deejaying, incorporating what I learned from other DJs into my own skill set —practicing what worked and trying to avoid what didn't. I worked really hard, and before long, I got good enough to get some real club gigs.

After spinning for a couple of months at the Laugh Factory, I started to deejay at other comedy clubs around town like the Comedy Store and Ha Ha Café. Most of the time it was the same thing that I was doing at Laugh Factory, but I was starting to build up my experience and my reputation. I continued to master the basics and soon moved on to real deejaying, where I could actually use the art of mixing to continuously play songs.

Karen spins at the Comedy Store

Before long, word got around about me. Working in the comedy clubs also built up my confidence and got me to the point where I really felt comfortable behind the turntables in front of crowds. I knew it wouldn't be long before I was ready to move on to bigger things and to challenge myself a little more. Of course, that meant spinning at the dance clubs where I had learned so much. I needed to be where the crowds were a little bit pickier about their music, where the DJ really had creative control. By then, I knew things were going to change. I was still going to school, but there was no turning back. I had fallen in love for the first time in my life and I wasn't going to break it off so easily this time.

Chapter 7:

Much Ado About Nothing

Looking back at that time in my life, it's interesting to see that as soon as I started to explore my surroundings and what life had to offer, things really started to blossom for me. Doors opened left and right; opportunities kept presenting themselves. Plus I was having fun! It was as if life had just been waiting for me to put myself out there and pursue what I really loved. As soon as I took those risks, one good thing would lead to another good thing. Even when situations didn't turn out so well, at the very least, I always learned lessons.

A guy named Judah Jackson saw me spin at the Laugh Factory. It turned out his brother was a well-known DJ in Los Angeles called DJ Bull. Judah asked me if I wanted to work a promotional event for Nike called the Nike People's Jam. I had only been deejaying for a short time, but I jumped at the offer. I'd be getting free gear and a paycheck, plus I knew it would be a good learning experience, and what the heck—it was Nike!

NIKE turntables

The Nike People's Jam was a month-long gig that toured around the high schools in the Los Angeles area. Every other day, we promoted Nike's different sneaker lines with the help of music and celebrities like Snoop Dogg. I was to provide the music out of a cool, classic convertible car from the 1970s. The trunk opened up to reveal a complete DJ station with turntables, lined with pink leopard-print faux fur. It was a really fun event, with music pumping through the air and the emcee passing out free Nike swag. I got on the turntables and started spinning background music when someone showed up with cameras and spotlights. The local news was covering the event and had decided that I was newsworthy. But as soon as the press showed up, Judah changed. He started hassling me about my deejaying, trying to point out my inexperience. He kept asking me if I had this that or that other record, and I said no. My record collection was pretty small because I was just starting out.

Of course, he got frustrated. And when he saw that the cameras were on me, he pushed me aside and started deejaying himself. I was shocked. Hadn't he recruited *me* to be the DJ? I knew his brother was a DJ and I also knew that Judah had some DJ experience, but really, this was just rude. I was pissed. Not knowing what else to do, I picked up some flyers and started handing them out. That's what I ended up doing for the rest of the tour. After all, I tried to rationalize, Judah got me the gig, so I guess he had the right to take it from me. I still got paid an hourly rate as a street team member. It was frustrating, but a learning experience about how quickly people can change when the cameras start to roll.

Plus, it led to more work for the next few years. Before the tour ended, I met the marketing company behind Nike's People Jam, Urban Marketing Corporation of America (UMCA). I took the initiative to walk right up to them and introduce myself. We exchanged cards and the next summer, they hired me to deejay another Nike event, the Nike Battleground Basketball tournament at Venice Beach. The Battleground event lasted for eight weeks during the summer, with street ball greats like Kareem Abdul-Jabbar, Jr. and the R&B singer Brian McKnight. It was another fun event, during which I spun background music to get the crowd and the players pumped up during the game. It just felt like one big summer block party. I went on to work Battleground events for the next three summers.

• •

Those gigs were more like parties than work for me. I couldn't believe people would basically pay me to have a lot of fun doing what I love to do. After a year with the turntables, I started getting real club gigs, where my music was the focus instead of being in the background. Tanya and I were at one of many clubs one night when she met a promoter named Joey King from King Entertainment. They started talking and she found out that he was looking for a DJ to open for a new club night at a popular Hollywood bar called Barfly. They wanted me to play the first half of the night, from 9 until about 11 p.m., just to warm up the crowd for the main headliner, DJ Florin, who would spin the prime-time hours, when the crowd really got going.

DJ Florin & Shy

At Barfly, the DJ booth was at the top of the club near the ceiling, somewhat hidden from the dance floor. I had to climb a ladder to get up there. I would go up first, then have some guys help lift up all my crates while I'd pull everything up myself. At first, I wondered why they had to make it so difficult for the DJ to get up to the booth. But then I realized that it was better that people couldn't see me. The crowd that came out to Barfly on Monday nights was predominantly black and they really knew their hip-hop and R&B. The first few times I deejayed, I was so nervous. I felt really intimidated because I was still trying to hone my mixing skills. Until then, I'd only deejayed for stand-up comics. It was a simple matter of hitting the play button and the stop button. But for clubs, I had to play songs back to back for hours. That meant I had to mix well too, especially for this outspoken and well-versed crowd.

Monday nights at Barfly became a very exclusive club night in L.A. because of the music industry. Record albums are usually released on a Tuesday, so on Monday nights before a record dropped, we'd get high-end, very exclusive clientele from the various record labels: Jive, Virgin, Interscope, Def Jam, Sony, Universal, etc. Artists like Jay-Z, Ludacris, Lil' Jon, Too Short, and plenty others came out and partied at Barfly. Needless to say, the crowd—all in the entertainment industry—was pretty sophisticated. They knew their music. They definitely wanted to hear the hits—*their* hits. There's nothing worse than seeing a bunch of people leaving the dance floor to sit down because the music sucked.

When deejaying for the dance floor, it's all about creating a mood and evoking an emotion. For those two hours, I had to learn how to control the little crowd I got. The hardest is always trying to lure people onto the dance floor in the beginning of the night. The hits had to be reserved for DJ Florin to spin during the prime time hours, so I had to come up with alternatives. I would start off slow, with some R&B music, while people got their drinks and started to relax. Then I would move into some old school Bel Biv Devoe, or West Coast rap, like Snoop Dogg or Ice Cube, and the clubbers would start getting excited and yell, "Aaaah! I love this song!" I knew they were reminiscing about when they were teenagers, hanging with their crew, or listening to this song on the radio when they first went out with their boyfriends. We all have those songs that make us go back in time, put us in a good mood, and make us go crazy on the dance floor. The power of good music can be intoxicating.

Week after week, I'd play. It wasn't long before I got really good at reading the crowd. Each week, I'd get a feel for the crowd and soon, I could point out all the regulars. I knew what they liked and what they didn't like. The crowd kept me on my toes. Then the music itself challenged me. I got to know the music I had in my small crate so well that I started getting sick of it. I wanted to change things up from my usual hip-hop playlist. I got hungry for more. I wanted to know everything about all the genres. I wanted to be able to grab a record and know exactly which songs to mix with what, like second nature. So I started asking around. I asked everyone—my friends, the bouncers, or other people who hung around the club. Growing up without any exposure to popular culture, I must have sounded pretty clueless. But back then, in my mind, I had a goal and to reach that goal, I would have to do some research. They told me about funk music: Tina Marie, Gap Band, George Clinton, and The Commodores. They listed which songs were their favorites, and I would write it all down and take my little list to the record store. I listened to them all and got to know them like old friends. After I learned about funk, I wanted to spin reggae, then old school, then East Coast hip-hop, then West Coast and so on. My curiosity never waned. In my head I would unravel the layers, take out the vocals, take out the strings and listen for those snares. Like the keyboard, I would be able to layer the beats of the next song and mix virtually any song with a beat. I knew these records would form the anchor for my collection and that I would have them forever. The classics never go out of style.

I learned fast and started rising even faster. My collection of music grew. Pretty soon I was able to mix hip-hop with rock, house with R&B, '80s with Top 40. It wasn't long before people started to take notice and my crowd changed. Pretty soon, white, Asian, and Hispanic crowds rolled through. There was nothing better than seeing a crowd get into what I was doing. I would just play and play, and the time would just fly by. When I deejayed at Barfly, no one could see me, so the only thing anyone could judge me by was the music I played and my mixing skills. It's funny how music brings people together. People started coming up to me after my set, shocked to see a woman—and an Asian woman at that—climbing down from the DJ booth. They would say, "Was that you up there? Great job!" And I would feel so proud to say yes. It was an awesome feeling.

In a couple of months, I got so good at spinning and working the crowd that the club promoters switched DJ Florin and me around—now he would open and I would be up there as the headliner. That felt especially good. When I first started, there just weren't very many women who deejayed, let alone Asian women, particularly anyone of Korean descent. I originally saw being an Asian female as a barrier to deejaying, but I learned to embrace my difference and let my skills speak for myself. When I saw that the crowd, especially a hard-core hip-hop crowd, liked what I was mixing and they went out of their way to tell me, I finally felt validated. So when I met people at the club, it was with pride that I told them that I was the DJ. That's what happened with a man named Don Price.

I remember when I first met him — it was a chilly night in mid-October. I went on the patio for a breather after I finished my set. I was standing near the wall, and I saw a group of friends, standing in a circle. He stood out among them; he was kind of short, with light mocha skin, and curly hair. He wasn't the hottest guy I'd ever seen, but there was something about him though. He was magnetic. He caught me looking, smiled, and started to walk toward me. He had a big grin on his face.

Don Price – Photography by Chris Ellin

"Hey, how ya doing?" he said.

"Hey." *Here we go*, I thought. I smiled gamely.

"I'm Don. You here with your friends?" he said.

"Nope. I'm one of the DJs," I said.

"Get out of here!"

"No really. I just finished my set."

"But you seem so bashful," he replied. "You totally don't fit the whole DJ profile."

We went back and forth for a while. He still thought I was kidding him. His god brother was head of security at Barny and wanted to give Don a taste of Hollywood nightlife. I gave him my number, and he made me promise that we would hang out next week. Every time he called to hang out though, I had to cancel on him. I felt horrible, because he thought I was playing him. But I had gigs that kept coming up and I couldn't turn them down.

Don & Karen with Shaq at Barfly

He still didn't even believe I was a DJ either. So to prove it to him, I invited him out to where I was filming an infomercial for a record store. When he arrived on set, he was really impressed, and almost shocked, that I could work the ones and twos. Afterwards, we went to go grub, and I finally got a chance to sit down and really talk with him. He was real cool — funny, and a little bit crazy. He kept making me laugh, and I noticed he was extremely charismatic and athletic, which I liked. He had even been a background dancer at one time for 'N SYNC. We talked about our families and our backgrounds. It turned out he had been raised by his mom, just like me. After my dad left us when I was ten, I'd never found anyone who had grown up fatherless and without much money too. Don and I connected instantly.

After a month of hanging out, we started dating. We spent a lot of time together in those days, talking about everything from music to work, family and friends. He expanded my growing repertoire of music, and in turn, I showed him what deejaying was all about. He would come with me to gigs and help me carry records and set up heavy equipment. Together, we saw many crazy things. I know Don thought I was dealing with some "shady" characters on the club scene, but I was just interested in the learning experience. I really didn't notice many of the things that were going on. Don tried to tell me, but I was pretty naïve. For instance, while spinning at Barfly, I met some friends of the promoters who set the club up on Monday nights. They hired me to work a mansion party in Malibu. They said they loved me because I was so different; I was a young Asian woman who knew my hip-hop. They thought that would add a new and different element to the party.

Don and I packed up to go to the party. We parked in a little strip mall and then took a shuttle up this long, narrow road into the hills. The mansion was beautiful and stood perched on a bluff overlooking the water. It was owned by a wealthy Japanese man named Mike who occasionally rented out the place to club promoters. They charged the people who wanted to come, and the owner made a cut of the door sales. Don helped carry my crates of records and turntables and helped set up all my equipment. As soon as I was all set, I started spinning, totally engrossed in the music. People started coming through the door and soon the party swelled to some 250 partygoers.

We were up on the balcony, overlooking the expansive living room. I could see that the party was pretty big, so I concentrated on the music. Don didn't have much to do, so he checked out the party scene and explored the ten-bedroom house. But he wasn't gone long before he came back with a worried look on his face. He told me the guys who hired me to deejay were taking men and women into the bedrooms. More girls kept arriving, and he was convinced that they were prostitutes. He said he saw money changing hands and people doing drugs.

I brushed him off. "No way. You're just paranoid," I said, continuing to spin. I didn't believe him. He was a couple years younger than me and didn't know anything about the DJ world. I was sure he was wrong. Why would these guys hire a DJ for prostitutes? Besides, they were paying me well—a couple hundred bucks for a couple hours' worth of work—and I needed the money. So I just put my headphones on and did my job. Don had no choice but to sit there and wait until the party ended.

After that day, they hired me to do a few more parties at the same mansion. It was steady work, and I was happy to add even more experience to my DJ resume. But eventually, Don and I noticed that the crowds at these parties started to dwindle. Don was still suspicious about the whole thing and voiced his opinions every once in a while. "Why are these guys paying you this money to come deejay for just a few people?" he'd always ask, and I could never answer him. By the last party I deejayed, there were only about 30 people there. When I had a free moment, I took a break from my booth and headed up to the balcony to take a look around. There were clouds of smoke and a nasty stench in the air. I couldn't believe I hadn't noticed it before. Everyone was high and smashed. There were some pretty skanky looking women lounging around, and I could clearly see all the drugs. I looked over at Don, who by this time, was kind of numb to this stuff and was playing with his Gameboy. "Don," I said to him, "I think you're right." We got out of there fast.

Even though Don was younger than me, and I thought less experienced, he turned out to be right about a lot of things. He never said so, but I suspect that he kept accompanying me to all these gigs because he wanted to protect me. And I guess he had good reason to. Even at Barfly, the promoters would pay the staff hundreds of bucks at the start of the evening. Then they would pay me at the end of the night—just $60 to $80. Don said this was unfair. He told me to speak up about it, but I thought I was still learning and they were giving me a break—like an unpaid intern, except I was fortunate that they were paying me at all. Don also had a problem with the fact that I had to pay for valet for a year while spinning at Barfly. It was only $10, but he felt I should've parked for free like the rest of the employees. Looking back, I guess he had a point.

Don really put up with a lot because he cared for me. I spun at many gay parties, and I never told Don beforehand because I knew he wouldn't come. When we were there, all sorts of guys would be tonguing each other, and sometimes they would try to rub up against Don.

One night, after I'd finished my set at Barfly, Don and I were packing my equipment into my car at the back of the club when we were approached by a young woman. She was well put together and dressed in designer clothes. She asked if we could drive her around to the front of the club to meet her friends. I figured she was drunk and wanted to give her a ride. She got into the car and we started driving toward the front of the club, but before we got there, she changed her story and said her pals had ditched her—could we take her back to her hotel right down the street? I asked Don if that was cool and he said yes, so we drove her to the Roosevelt Hotel. She kept telling us how nice we were and insisted that she take us out for a meal to thank us. Don and I were tired, so we declined. We pulled up to the hotel and instead of saying goodbye, she told us that she might be at the wrong hotel and needed to go to the Argyle instead. She asked us to wait while she ran inside and came back out with a Louis Vuitton duffle bag. As we continued on to the Argyle, she told us stories about how she came from a wealthy family in Europe and was just visiting, yet she seemed to know exactly where we were going and kept telling Don which streets to take. Then she asked us to drive her to another hotel on Hollywood Boulevard because she had to make a quick stop. The minute she left the car and ran inside with the duffle, Don flipped out. We'd been driving all over Los Angeles late at night with a stranger who kept changing her story and asking us to make stops. This last stop put him over the edge. He dumped her purse out on the sidewalk and we drove off. I was upset and felt terrible that we were leaving this girl all by herself without any transportation. "Karen, we could've been transporting drugs!" Don said to me. "Or maybe she's a hooker."

Looking back, I was pretty naïve. Whether or not that woman was telling the truth, Don was right—we should've been more careful. I was flirting with danger without even knowing it; I guess I was pretty gullible. And then to top it off, during the summer of 2004, I got a phone call that led to the craziest gig yet.

"Hey Karen, are you free next Saturday?" It was Judah—the same guy who had gotten me the Nike gig. He said there was a house party in Compton and asked if I could deejay for him because he couldn't make it. I said sure—I was excited to go to the infamous city of Compton because it was mentioned in a lot of movies and songs. Don thought differently. He knew the neighborhood where the party was because it was right down the street from his uncle's barbershop. He told me it was on the dividing line between Bloods and Crips territory. A lot of kids down there were involved with gangs and would start trouble in his uncle's barbershop. Needless to say, his radar was on high alert, and he was very anxious about me spinning at a house party in that area. He told me to forget it. I thought he was being silly—paranoid and overreacting. I was excited about it.

We drove out there and came up to a modest house. A nice couple was celebrating their niece's high school graduation. There were about 50 high school kids hanging out on the front lawn. The family couldn't have been nicer—food was laid out for the kids and the whole thing seemed pretty chill. We set up and got to spinning. The party went off without a hitch and everyone was having a great time, enjoying the music. Afterwards, we started breaking down. I packed up and Don started carrying stuff back to the car. All of a sudden—BANG! I heard loud popping noises and lots of loud, excited voices. Don came running around the side of the house toward me, yelling at me.

"GET IN THE HOUSE!" he screamed at me. The owners of the house came running out, frantically telling everyone to get inside. I didn't understand what all the commotion was about. I thought somebody was putting off firecrackers.

"I want to see!" I told Don. He yelled at me to get down. Soon, I heard the wail of sirens getting louder and the sound of screeching tires just outside the house. I then understood that something was very wrong.

Apparently, two groups of kids had gotten into an argument on the front lawn during the party. Don was going around the side of the house where there was a gate and a little path to the front yard when he saw a car racing in reverse down the street. Two kids were hanging out of the side windows, waving guns. They started shooting. The car was flying towards the front lawn of the house, bouncing off parked cars lining both sides of the street. The kids on the front lawn started shooting back. Everyone scattered. It was chaos. When it was finally safe to come out, the entire block had been cordoned off, and big policemen in S.W.A.T. gear were standing around, interviewing people.

We were stuck in Compton until 4 o'clock in the morning. Don was so pissed. "I told you," he kept saying to me again and again on the way home. He said he knew something wasn't right when no cops came after 11 o'clock. "Any normal place and the cops come after 11 p.m. if you got the music cranked," he said. We were spinning music loud well after 1 a.m. and no one had complained. We found out later that the party was not for a graduation at all. It turned out that the nice couple often threw illegal parties where kids paid a $5 cover and paid for alcohol. It was like an underground club for teens. We also discovered that two groups of kids had been hassling each other throughout the night at the party. The whole thing just exploded out on the front yard as things were breaking up.

• •

Not all the events we did were so extreme, though. There were plenty of tame and legit gigs, too. Don and I spun at fashion shows, and we provided music at a hip-hop clothing store in the Beverly Center called Up Against the Wall. Through it all, we became very close. I felt comfortable enough around Don to really open up to him. I told him everything about my family and where I grew up. He knew how hard my mom pushed me to "be somebody": a doctor, a lawyer. She had such a difficult life in America, and she wanted to protect me from that same fate. I wanted something different for myself. I was determined to make it on my own terms. Maybe that's why I put up with so much of the craziness I experienced deejaying.

Don Price & Karen Beck

We dated for two years, Don and I. But in the end, the life that I was leading was too much for him to handle. All those late nights, the shady characters, the hustling to get paid. And there were also the phone calls from strange guys, stalkers—the ones I gave my phone number to because they said they wanted to help me, or work with me, or any number of reasons—but really they only wanted to get with me and kept harassing me late at night with phone calls. All that found their way into the space between me and Don. Eventually, we broke up. But now we have a real friendship. To this day, he still looks out for me and keeps me balanced. He is my best friend.

Chapter 8:

The Business

Nightclubs in L.A. come and go with about a two-year lifespan. There are so many clubs in Hollywood that the venues constantly undergo renovation or go under new ownership just to keep up with competition. Eventually, the buzz around Barfly died down, and soon it wasn't the hot spot anymore. I knew good gigs like that couldn't last forever, but when it finally happened, I freaked out. I started searching for another regular DJ gig everywhere I could. In my desperation, I frantically flipped through the Yellow Pages, looking up various nightclubs to apply to, when suddenly an idea dawned upon me. What if I took an ad out to advertise my deejaying services?

I immediately contacted the advertising department at the Greater Los Angeles Yellow Pages to inquire about getting some space. Luckily, there was one spot left to fill in the DJ services section. The man on the phone had to get rid of that spot by a certain deadline or else they would have to somehow fill up that space, so he sold it to me for a great deal. The ad was eye-catching and colorful, and in big letters it read, "ONE STOP DJ CONNECTION: providing music for weddings, birthdays & events." It had a big red stop sign as my logo. It was definitely the first thing that would catch your eye before any other competing advertisements, especially since all the other ads were in black and white. Lastly, with the money I saved from spinning, I invested in speakers, flashing colored strobe lights, microphones, and fog machines. Don became my partner, and together we found ourselves running a mobile DJ business.

Not long after I placed the ad, dozens of calls started pouring in with all kinds of requests — high school proms, weddings, birthdays, bar mitzvahs, and quinceañeras. My first caller asked if I had reggae as well as Klezmer, a type of Yiddish music that sounds kind of like Jewish jazz. I had no idea what they were talking about, but I said yes to everything. Since it was our first call, we didn't want to turn anything down, but Don had some doubts that I'd be able to get the 13-year-old teenage boys to move.

When we arrived at the Sherwood Country Club in Westlake Village, I was amazed at its splendor. The golf course was a sprawling, manicured expanse of green grass. It was the same place where Tiger Woods played the ProAm golf tournament every year. I left my car with valet and walked inside the banquet room. Don was right behind me with my records — Top 40, hip-hop, and R&B in the pink camouflage case, and my rock music in the black bag. Some of the kids were there already, with their little yarmulkes pinned atop their head onto their short, spiky hair. More and more people filtered into the room until there were hundreds of parents and kids assembled, ready to party. This was really different than I was used to at Barfly, but I decided to roll with it. I set up and played some mellow pop while the crowd got warmed up. At 9 p.m., the guests finished dinner, and according to tradition we were supposed to do the chair dance. I didn't have the Hebrew chair song, so I put on some Pit Bull, a fast, hard-hitting reggae song, and the crowd went wild. The boys started to break dance, and the girls danced in a line. When the time came around for the chair dance, the boy of honor sat on one of the gilded chairs while his friends and family hoisted him up. I didn't have the proper bar mitzvah music, but by that time no one cared— they bounced that boy to manhood to Snoop Dogg and Pharrell's "Drop It Like It's Hot." I had done it! I had made them fall in love with the music. The event coordinator handed me $500 at 1 a.m., and we called it a night. Don was shocked — we had earned about $125 an hour just for playing records.

The next morning, still glowing from the success of my first mobile DJ gig, I decided to call my mom and share my experience with her.

"Hey, Mom, guess what!"

"What?"

"I made $500 last night from my DJ business!"

"What?" she said. "DJ? That is bad! DJ no good — dancing, smoking, drinking, boys— NO!" She immediately started interrogating me on how I began, how long I'd been spinning for, where I'd been spinning, who I'd been influenced by, etc. I tried reassuring her that there was just more to deejaying than the clubs. I thought she would be proud that I opened a little business just like her. Instead, I opened Pandora's Box. She started calling me on a daily basis to check up on what I was doing, if I was still in school, if I needed money. It felt like I'd gone back to living in her house in high school. She figured I was doing it because I was desperate for money. She even offered to buy my turntables from me in an attempt to get me to stop.

Karen graduates USC

Ultimately, my mom was worried that deejaying would affect my studies at USC. Even though my grades were not as good as they'd been at Penn State and high school, I still passed my classes. It was the summer before I was required to complete a full year of residency of working full-time in the health administration field before getting my degree. All I could think of was how much fun I had spinning and the great money I'd been making from it. But I also reminisced about my summer in Korea and its nightlife. I wanted to take advantage of my last real summer before I'd have to enter the workforce and forever be a slave to a corporate job. I wanted to deejay overseas.

I figured if the Yellow Pages ads had worked to get me business in the Los Angeles, area, maybe advertising on the Internet would help me reach a wider global audience. I went online and set up a musician's profile on MySpace promoting my DJ services. To make my profile stand out, I did everything I could to enhance it—I added videos, samples of my mixes, photos, and anything else that would attract people to book me. I started searching MySpace for club owners, club managers, and promoters in Asia so I could add them to my friends. Before I knew it, I had over 1,000 friends. My fan base was steadily increasing, as were my bookings.

To my surprise, a club manager from Taipei, Taiwan, contacted me out of the blue. They wanted me to take a red-eye flight to get to Taipei the following week and offered to pay for my flight and hotel expenses. I was ecstatic—it was my first DJ gig overseas! At the Taipei International Airport, I was greeted by a girl named Carol, who would be my guide and translator during the duration of my stay. We hopped into a limo and checked in at the luxurious Imperial Hotel. Over the next few days, Carol became my personal guide, chauffeuring me around Taipei and translating everything into English. Together, we explored all types of markets, restaurants, shops, and historic sights. It was a real adventure.

DJ Shy spinning at Ministry of Sound in Taipei, Taiwan

The manager set me up to spin at a club in Taipei called M.O.S. (Ministry of Sound) for four nights, performing Wednesday, Thursday, Friday, and Saturday. The world-famous club was enormous and British-owned. The venue was especially known for flying in a diverse array of renowned musicians from all over. They brought in DJs from all over the world like Boy George, Jazzy Jeff, Paul Oakenfold, Sasha, and WhooKid. It was an honor to perform on the same stage as these legends.

When I played there, they had a main dance floor that held about 2,000 people, all dancing to trance and electronica beats. I was hired to play the hip-hop room, which held about 500 partiers. It was a crazy experience. The technology at the club was unlike anything I'd seen, with huge pyrotechnics right inside the club. It was so much more advanced compared to what we had here in the States. The lights, the smoke system—it just blew me away. The crowd was predominantly young and very appreciative. Their non-stop energy and enthusiasm for the music and the clubbing scene was something I'd never really seen in the States. It felt great to be a part of it.

After my set, I met DJ agents Richard Wan and Ricky Stone from RnR Asia, who said they wanted to sign me to a contract and send me on a tour through some Asian cities. It was a dream come true. Still, because my previous experiences with Don had taught me some lessons, I had some initial reservations. Since this was my first contract, I took some time to read it over carefully and think about it, even though the term was only for six months. I wanted to make sure that I would still have my freedom during that time and they wouldn't "own" me or anything. After all I'd been through, who knew what would come up during those six months? When I got back to the States, I felt pretty comfortable that I would be okay, so I signed with RnR Asia and they sent me off on a two-week tour during the holidays through some of Asia's biggest cities. And as it turned out, I really didn't have to worry.

• •

Asia was a whirlwind. I plane-hopped from city to city the whole time. My first stop was Beijing, China. I was there to spin at a venue next to the old Olympic Stadium called Club Mix for one night only.

Club Mix in Beijing

As soon as the night was over, I boarded another plane to Bangkok to spin at Q Bar. Just a few hours later, I was on another plane to Singapore to spin at Cocco Latte. I was able to spend a couple days in Shanghai, where I spun at Lux. I finally ended the tour in Hong Kong, spinning at C Club, Lux, and California Club. It was all a blur, but one thing that struck me was that Asia was a giant mix of contrasts. One minute I was in the middle of a huge modern city; the next, I felt like I'd traveled back centuries.

DJ Shy spinning at Cocco Latte in Singapore

Beijing Soldiers – Photography by August Jackson

While everything seemed to go by so fast, Beijing in particular was a major culture shock. I remember seeing a group of soldiers marching through the park. They were so stiff, walking in perfect unison. Dressed in their green uniforms and red armbands with a rifle by their side, they moved together as one unit, marching in sync with staccato rhythms. Seeing soldiers marching in a lush, green park, where kids, old people, and everyone else were going about their everyday business like it was no big deal, was totally surreal to me. It was nothing like I'd seen in America.

In hot and humid Bangkok, I rode a tuk tuk, a makeshift taxi that looks like the back half of a buggy mashed together with the front half of a motorcycle. The ride was fast and dusty. I was mesmerized by how these tuk tuk drivers navigated the maze of streets through all the traffic and chaos of the city.

Singapore was the complete opposite. It almost felt like there was no dust at all in Singapore. I wanted to run a white-gloved finger along the sidewalks to see. The city was so clean and spotless, even gum-chewing is banned for fear of sullying up the sidewalks. They had a red light district, and yet you couldn't chew gum. Coming from America, I just couldn't understand that kind of a contradiction.

Hong Kong - Photography by © Leung Cho Pan

Hong Kong was the most modern of all the Asian places I visited. The city was like a glimpse into the future. Tall, shiny buildings rose up all around me, their reflections mirrored in the bay that surrounded the island. The streets were crowded with well-dressed people rushing to and from work, and the food was incredible. Life was brimming from every corner in Hong Kong. It was like a glitzy, Asian Manhattan, especially the area I was staying in, Lan Kwai Fong. That attitude pervaded even in the clubs. The club crowds where I spun were dressed to the nines. People were very conservative, but they knew how to flash the bling.

In Shanghai, I actually had a few days to explore. Compared to Hong Kong, Shanghai was like a blast from the past. The city was such an interesting mix of old and new. Some unassuming buildings looked like they had been there for centuries. I half expected someone from the seventeenth century to walk out at any minute. Pieces of history were visible all throughout the city, and then around the corner, you'd see modern buildings and houses. The city center was a mash up of neon lights and flashing signs. It looked like New York's Times Square times ten.

But while it was clear that Shanghai was flexing its economic muscles, there were signs of poverty that were only made starker in contrast to the shiny buildings and bright lights. There were a lot of poor people in Shanghai, and they weren't like the homeless population I'd seen in LA. One night, after my set, I was heading back to my hotel at about 3 or 4 in the morning. It was drizzling a little bit and I was running and dodging the rain, when I came across a woman holding a child. The child looked weak, like he was sick and dying. He was just lying in this woman's arms, limp. She held out her hands and asked for money. I couldn't help but think about where I'd come from. I knew what it was like to struggle without money. This child could have had a father somewhere, who maybe was doing alright, but for whatever reason, wasn't living up to his responsibilities to help his own child. I noticed there were many kids in Shanghai who would run out and beg for money or whatever you had. But I didn't have anything to give them.

• •

Montreal – Photography by Daryl Fritz

My foray into the international music scene didn't stop at Asia. My next stop after the Asian tour was Montreal, Canada. Montreal was the complete polar opposite of Asia. For one thing, almost everywhere I looked there were blonde, blue-eyed people. Unlike Asia's neon lights and skyscrapers, Montreal's atmosphere was quaint; while Asia was mostly hot and humid, Montreal was chilly and beautiful. The streets were made of cobblestone, and everywhere you walked you could hear the fluid sounds of French being spoken. When I first met the promoters who hired me, they kissed me on both cheeks. I was taken aback, but then they explained that this was how the French greeted each other—with a "bisou bisou," which literally means "kiss kiss."

From there, they had a white stretch limo whisk me off to the club. The first was Super 9, a really fun, loud club filled with lots of college students. The club goers looked American to me, like Abercrombie models, but everyone spoke French. The second night, a Hummer picked me up to spin at an afterhours spot called Circus. It was located downtown and had an underground vibe to it. The rest of my time in Montreal I spent walking around by myself, just window shopping and taking it all in. As I strolled down the cobblestone streets, I thought about how much my life had changed in just a few short years. I thought about where I'd been and where I was going. It had been such a short time since I had decided to go full time with my deejaying, and yet, here I was, traveling all over the world, meeting new people, seeing new sights, and experiencing different worlds. Cooped up in my house in New Castle, I never imagined that the world was as big as it is. Now, as I walked around, I felt the joy of freedom in everything I was experiencing—the brisk, cold air, the French being spoken all around me, the clean streets. All the uncertainty I had felt before when I was still juggling my gigs and my daytime job just melted away. I took in the scenery and thought about the future. I was never more certain about my belief in what I was meant to do.

But when I arrived back in LA, I had to come down from the high of traveling and my intense schedule of working night after night. I had to come back to reality. I was about to enter into the workforce.

Chapter 9:
Residency

I found a paid residency that combined my knack for numbers and my affection for kids at the Children's Hospital of Los Angeles' orthopedics department. I worked from 8 until 5, Monday through Friday. My main responsibilities were working as a secretary for Dr. Skaggs, a renowned orthopedics surgeon who writes books and tours the country lecturing about his work. While taking care of Dr. Skaggs' schedule and appointments, my work was split between a billing manager named Rosalia, the division administrator, Diane, and the hospital's operations manager, Mary. I juggled many responsibilities for my many superiors, but I handled it pretty well.

KIIS FM logo

During down time, I'd sit in the office I shared with two other surgeon's secretaries, Lydia and Julissa. There was a small, beat-up radio in the office that was always tuned to 102.7 KIIS FM. I started looking forward to listening to Ryan Seacrest and Ellen K in the mornings when I first arrived. Then I learned that Lydia's son, Ricky, worked at KIIS FM in the promotions department. Lydia would always talk about how much Ricky loved working at the radio station—how it was such a fun and exciting place to work. She always beamed with pride whenever she talked about what her son did. On-air personality Jo-Jo had become a family friend of theirs, often coming over to Lydia's house for dinner. KIIS was a top national radio station, so I couldn't help but feel impressed with all her stories.

Previously my station of choice had been Power 106; I listened daily to Big Boy's neighborhood morning shows. The station had a variety of different DJs scratch, mix, and spin the music live on air while the hosts talked. KIIS had just started following a similar format, with DJ Drew spinning the noon mix of hip-hop, rock, Top 40, and pop music. I remember spending my mornings and afternoons in that office, listening to Lydia's stories and the tiny sounds of that beat-up little radio playing all the tunes from KIIS. Instead of being background music, the radio became all I could hear. It made me daydream about how much I wanted to work at a place like KIIS.

My schedule was pretty hectic working 8 to 5 at the hospital, plus spinning at the clubs three nights a week. But no matter how tired I was, hearing that radio and Lydia talk always motivated me to apply for a job at KIIS. I managed to find time to record a demo CD and put together a resume with a list of upcoming gigs. I sent it all to KIIS FM along with my application for the on-air mixer position.

Six months quickly passed with no word from anyone at KIIS. I was happy enough working at Children's Hospital and settling into my new apartment, which I shared with Don in Los Feliz. While I was working, Don had gotten a job in retail at Circuit City next door, so moving in together made sense. But in the back of my mind, I was always hoping the phone would ring, and it would be KIIS calling to offer me a job.

Before long, my residency ended and I moved on to a higher-paying, full-time job with a consulting firm. The job involved a lot of travel, which was exciting. The company sent me to New York City to do some work at Cedars Sinai Hospital. Knowing I was going to be in NYC, I made some calls and was able to book some DJ gigs out there during my business trip. While I went from day to day working the consulting job, my heart was in spinning music.

After many months, I still hadn't heard anything from KIIS, but I was determined not to give up. I updated my resume and sent it to the music director a second time. I included an updated list of upcoming gigs to show that I was in demand, as well as another demo CD.

Meanwhile, I was slowly letting people on to my "secret life" at work. Lots of people say that you should never mix your business with your personal life, but I couldn't help but befriend my new coworkers and invite them to parties where I was spinning. It wasn't long before the entire office found out that I deejayed on nights and weekends. The problem with letting my coworkers know more about me was that it invited people into my private life, which opened the door to some problems. For example, the owner of my firm started taking a great deal of interest in me. I'd come into the office in the morning and find 2-pound bags of my favorite candy, peanut M&Ms, on my desk that he would "surprise" me with for all to see. He'd invite me to go to meetings with him even though this meant I couldn't get my own work done. He also tried to help me get a new apartment close by in South Pasadena and insisted on telling me stories about how his wife had recently undergone surgery to combat breast cancer. Naturally, my coworkers thought all the attention from the company's owner was very strange. One coworker in particular, a young guy named Elliot, used to make wry comments about how fond the boss man was of me.

With all that drama at work, I decided I needed to leave quickly—so I found a better, higher paying job with a company called Universal Health Care in Long Beach. The job carried more responsibility. Even though my salary almost doubled, my commute was not easy. I had to get up at 5 o'clock in the morning and take a 45-minute Metro ride from South Pasadena all the way south to Long Beach. It meant me going back to public transportation and a daily trip through Compton.

My schedule started to get insane. I was working at the office Monday through Friday, and I was spinning Friday, Saturday, Sunday, and Monday nights. I was severely lacking in sleep and often nodded off during my commute, missing my train stop. I would gulp down two, three cups of coffee every morning to get myself going. The only way I could hang out with my friends was to invite them to come see me spin at the local clubs.

I was working myself to the bone, but I still hadn't heard anything from KIIS FM. It was frustrating. I swallowed my pride and figured that the third time was the charm. I updated my resume and upcoming events list and put it together with my best demo CD yet. I sent the whole package off to KIIS—yet again—with the hopes that I would finally hear from them.

In time, a rival company named Health Net bought Universal Health Care. This meant I was going to experience another downsize. With my unlucky history of getting downsized or having sleazy bosses, I felt like I just wasn't meant to work a corporate job. The company gave us six months notice to look for another job. In a panic, I quickly applied for the Ph.D. program at USC. This time, no luck.

With no back-up plan, there was no choice but to look for another job. Fortunately, I was hired at L.A. Care, which was located smack dab in the middle of the concrete sprawl of downtown L.A. It was a much easier commute, but in car-obsessed Los Angeles, there's no such thing as a real "easy" commute. Around the same time, I became the resident DJ at a club called Hurricane Bar in Huntington Beach. The club was a good 50 miles from my front door in South Pasadena, all the way down south, past Long Beach. I was really burning the candle on both ends, trying to juggle my day job and pursue my love of deejaying on weeknights and weekends.

Making two incomes was awesome. But, like before, the lack of sleep and running on empty all the time was really starting to kill me. I was exhausted all the time. I started making mistakes at my day job, and management started to notice. It was often tough to focus during my club gigs as well. Sometimes my mixes were off—I was stretched so thin that both my careers were suffering.

Soon after, I booked a gig spinning at a M.A.C. cosmetics event in Nordstrom's at The Grove on a Saturday afternoon. The Grove is an upscale outdoor mall built around the famous Farmer's Market, an L.A. landmark since Hollywood's heyday. It's situated right across from CBS studios and bordered by the Writer's Guild of America and trendy Melrose Avenue. After spinning for an hour or so, I noticed this hip, blonde, 20-something woman staring at me. It made me uncomfortable. In between songs, she approached me and said that she really dug my spinning—especially my technique in mixing the songs. I was surprised at that remark since most people don't even notice the subtle moves that go into mixing. The blonde woman went on to say that she wanted to find a way for us to work together. I didn't really know what that meant until she told me that she was Julie Pilat, the music director at KIIS FM. I was shocked. I had been trying to get someone—anyone—from KIIS FM to acknowledge me, and here the music director was in person, watching me spin! She took notice of the upcoming gigs listed on my resume and came down for a visit since she lived across the street. I was surprised as well to find that the music director was someone like Julie. I expected the music director at the number one radio station in America to be a 40-something corporate type in a fine suit with a Blackberry permanently fixed in one hand, not a friendly, young blonde woman in jeans. It was encouraging to know that someone in a position of power in the music industry was a young woman like myself, and I felt heartened by it.

Julie invited me to come down to the station so we could talk more about the possibility of working together. I was excited and nervous about the whole thing. She clearly liked my work behind the turntables, but that didn't mean I had the gig—my dream gig—at KIIS FM in the bag. At that point, all I knew was that she wanted to have a conversation.

Julie and I set a time for me to come down to the station. I took the day off from work. When I arrived at the station, I was nervous with anticipation. I couldn't help but think of all the musicians that walked through the same hallways—Madonna, Justin Timberlake, etc.—and here I was, following their footsteps. After we chatted for a little bit about the job, Julie started taking me around to everyone, introducing me as KIIS's newest on-air mixer. I met everyone, including Jo-Jo, whom I had heard so much about at Children's Hospital from Lydia. Slowly, my shock wore off and I realized that I had gotten the job on the spot! All my hard work had paid off—I was now a part of KIIS FM.

The station had two on-air mixers, and I was to be the third. This meant that my new job was to spin—just like I do during a club gig—except it would go on the radio for millions of people to hear. The on-air mixer would spin while the personality interacted with the listening audience. Mixers would go on air during lunch, from noon to 1 in the afternoon, Monday through Friday; during traffic hour, 5 to 6 on Friday afternoons; and during "club hours," from 10 at night until 2 in the morning on Friday and Saturday nights.

Though I technically had the job, there was still one more step I had to complete before I could feel absolutely secure about having the job. KIIS is a very family-oriented station, so any curse words would have to bleeped out of the music played on their airwaves. I soon learned that the most important part of my new job was to pre-record the mix that I planned to play on the air. The mix had to be approximately 45 minutes long and submitted to the station in advance before it could go on air. Julie gave me a week to do the mix. I was nervous because I had never mixed anything so complicated before. I had downloaded a free recording program from the Internet called Wave Lab to help create my demo CDs. Before this, the most sophisticated I'd ever gotten with Wave Lab was to use the play, stop, and record functions. I had no idea how to delete out certain words in songs or how to add in the KIIS FM sweepers—both vital parts of an on-air mix for any radio station.

I went home with one thought in my head: I've landed my dream gig…now I have to live up to it. I was determined to do it by myself and do it well, but it was a painstaking process to figure out how to use the Wave Lab program. I had two turntables for vinyl records and a third turntable to play CDs. I was juggling all three tables at the same time as I tried to lay the mix with the sweepers and make it as slick and tight as possible. For the next seven days, I barely got a wink of sleep. Any free time I had went into that mix CD. Making things more complicated was the fact that I had specific instructions on what kind of songs to play and what order they should follow for the mix, plus I had to leave room for 30-second talk breaks. On top of that, KIIS has a coding system for songs: An "A" song is a track that is brand new; a "B" song is a track that is less than six months old; an "S" song is a track that is a year old; and a "P" track is more than three years old. KIIS provided me with all the music to play, but I had to put them together in certain sequences—for example, the first 15 minutes of the mix had to contain two S tracks, one A track, and one B track.

Putting together the mix felt like trying to assemble a giant jigsaw puzzle in record time. It also became a real struggle to get the volume on the mix just right. All the songs had different volume levels, which I had to even out. Some were too low, others too loud. I kept at it and eventually got a handle on the Wave Lab program after a few days. My first mix wasn't perfect, but it impressed Julie enough to get it played on the air. I was beyond excited. I told all my friends and even my mom to tune in to KIIS the day my mix hit the airwaves. I had finally arrived.

Chapter 10:

KIIS This!

A few days after getting the job at KIIS, the reality of the situation finally began to settle in. I couldn't believe that I was now working at KIIS FM — ranked the number one radio station in America by Arbitron. Famous radio hosts like Rick Dees had built their careers at the radio station. Now their big name is Ryan Seacrest, who catapulted to an even higher level of fame as the host of the hit reality television show, *American Idol*. Just a year ago, I had been sitting in an office listening to KIIS and daydreaming about a job there, and now somehow, by perhaps some act of divine intervention, I was the one who was on the airwaves. Newly hired, I knew I had a big job ahead of me and I was truly excited.

My mind was racing with a rush of thoughts, sounds, and images of my life from the past years. I heard my mom, calling my name at Perkins; I heard the melody of my first Tina Marie song; I smelled the scent of Korea and I could see my dad, in his condo in Seoul; I remembered haggling with promoters to get paid, fights with my little brother; and how, my first time in a club in Korea, I could literally feel the music thumping through my chest. Now I knew what it felt like to hear my mix roll out on the radio on KIIS FM, to thousands of listeners. By all accounts I had traveled so far and was now living my dream.

Things easily could have gone the other way. What if I had never filled in for the other hostess at the Laugh Factory, or was too scared to follow through on that Asian tour contract? Or what if I had given up when I didn't hear back from KIIS after submitting my demo the second time? I was supremely thankful that somehow, I'd made it to where I was. In the days following the first time my mix aired on the radio, I felt like I could do anything.

Dream or no dream, the *reality* of my life quickly set in. It wasn't long before I realized that my schedule was completely overloaded. With working at KIIS, spinning on the weekends, and holding down an 8-to-5 office job, I barely slept and I found it hard not to make mistakes at work. Don and I decided not to renew the Yellow Pages ad for One Stop DJ Connection and put an end to the mobile deejaying business. I asked my boss if I could drop down to a part-time position at L.A. Care, but he oddly took that to mean that I didn't have enough to do, so he gave me even more work. Meanwhile, after hearing my first mix, Julie approved and asked for more. But I wasn't sure that I could deliver them on time. I'm not a quitter, but I was also trying to be realistic. I wanted to do a good job at both, but one was clearly winning out. I didn't know what to do.

I was also landing more and more high-profile gigs. By this time, I was a familiar face on the club scene. The more people heard and liked my music, the better the gigs I got. This opened up new opportunities for me, including spinning at red carpet events, a staple of Hollywood life. I remember when I first came to Los Angeles, I would drive down Hollywood Boulevard hoping to get a glance at the town's latest movie premiere. I loved observing all the fans and paparazzi taking photos as the movie stars walked by. It was so surreal to see something I had seen so many times on TV actually happening right in front of me in real life. It's hard not to get caught up in all the excitement, even as you're standing there, squeezed in elbow to elbow with hundreds of other fans, crushed into barricades, almost blinded by the constant popping of camera flashes. I had no clue that years later, I would no longer be standing on the outside, behind those barricades looking in; I was inside, spinning at the red carpet events, an arm's length away from those very same stars.

Coolio and DJ Shy at a KIIS event

The excitement outside those events was nothing compared to the excitement I felt inside. The first Hollywood event I spun at was for Samsung, hosted by Jeremy Piven, who at the time was one of the hottest actors thanks to the success of the HBO show, *Entourage.* The show was about a guy who achieves fame almost overnight and takes to the Hollywood life with his closest friends, something that I could very well imagine. The event featured a performance by actress/singer Taryn Manning. Among the well-heeled guests was the kitschy burlesque-turned-pop act, the Pussycat Dolls, as well as many other artists and actors. It felt great to be surrounded by creative people who were successful at their craft and to share my music with them.

DJ Shy & Kimberly from the Pussycat Dolls

I knew I had to make a decision. Spinning at KIIS was the chance of a lifetime — my dreams were just starting to become a reality. I knew I had to take that leap of faith, trust in myself, and concentrate on my DJ career full time. It was a difficult decision, especially when I was used to receiving a hefty check automatically every other week, along with health benefits and paid sick days. As uncertain and unpredictable as it was, as lofty and as unfamiliar as it was, especially to my mom and my upbringing, music was simply what I always wanted to do. And in that moment, as I was weighing these two sides of my life, I knew the right decision was right before me. I finally decided to leave my job at L.A. Care to devote my time to music and my job at KIIS.

I definitely had reservations about breaking the news about my decision to Mom. I understood how much she'd sacrificed to raise my brother and me. I knew how much she worried and watched over us. The last thing I wanted to do was disappoint her or make her feel like she'd failed in any way. Much to my surprise, when I told my mom about quitting my day job to deejay full-time, she completely changed her tune. Mom was very impressed with my new career choice at KIIS FM. She knew who Ryan Seacrest was and loved KIIS FM's family-oriented ethics. I was finally able to communicate my passion and determination to have a career as a DJ to her. My mom finally understood that working for KIIS FM was a once-in-a-lifetime opportunity and that I had to give it all my passion and energy to make it happen. Finally getting my mother's approval only reinforced the feeling that I was making the right decision.

When I decided to work full-time as a DJ, my mom told me, "You're a professional now." That really resonated with me. Coming from a successful professional herself—my mom single-handedly raised kids and built a business all by herself—that statement meant a lot to me. Just as my mom overcame all these odds being an Asian woman alone in a mostly white rural town in a country far from her home, I had defied obstacles facing me in the music scene, being an Asian American female DJ in a male-dominated business. My mom's approval emboldened me to follow in her footsteps and to make my business a success. When I did my first mix for KIIS FM, the first person I sent a copy to was my mom. She listened to the mix and called me first thing.

"Karen," she said over the phone, "I'm *so* proud of you." That meant the world to me.

It's not like it's been a walk in the park going full-time, either. I had some major adjustments to make. When I was working my office job, I would get up at 7 o'clock in the morning and get my day started. Now, I had no job to go to; I was my own boss. It was difficult to learn how to manage my time. I also had no one telling me what I supposed to do — I had to figure out how to run my new business all by myself.

DJ Shy's First Business License

In February of 2006, I got my first business license. I started contacting promoters and bookers and sifting through offers for new gigs. My overall goal was to get my name out there on a national level. Working towards this end, my publicist friend booked me at my first red carpet event. I was so excited when she told me I was going to walk the red carpet. I had gone from trying to catch a glimpse of these events, to working at them, to *walking* the carpet as an invited guest as many as four times a week — just to be seen out on the town and to network with the movers and shakers of the entertainment industry.

On the way to my first red carpet event, I reminisced about my days at USC. A friend of mine who worked in marketing at Paramount Pictures had access to movie premieres and after-party tickets. She gave me a pass to attend the movie premiere of *Guess Who*, starring Ashton Kutcher and Bernie Mac. I wanted to take my mom with me to the premiere so that she could experience Hollywood firsthand. When we got to the event, Mom and I realized that *all* guests and attendees of the premiere had to walk the red carpet in order to get into the iconic Mann's Chinese Theatre. I never thought little old me would be on the carpet, walking in the footsteps of all those celebrities. Even though the paparazzi were changing their lens and taking breaks while my mom and I walked through, I was exhilarated. I'd had a little taste of what it was like to be someone successful, appreciated, and loved, and I never forgot that feeling.

Now, I was in the back of a limousine crawling down Sunset Boulevard, on the way to my first red carpet event as DJ SHY. As the car pulled up to the event, I realized just how nervous I was. The event was being held to kick off the launch of ImaginAsian TV, the nation's first Asian American television network. Actors such as Leonardo Nam from *The Fast & The Furious*, Dante Basco from *Hook*, Dat Phan, winner of the reality television contest *Last Comic Standing*, and many others were waiting to get introduced by a bank of jostling, cell-phone juggling publicists to the press. When it finally came to my turn to be introduced, my knees almost buckled. The thing I remember most was the rush of sound — ten different camera guys calling my name, yelling for me to "look over here" at the same time. There was this constant din in the air — the combined whir of camera shutters and flash bulbs popping. I wasn't sure how to pose or what to say as I moved down the press line, the reporters putting their microphones in my face and expecting me to say something. Everyone was asking me about my outfit and who the designer was. I had no clue! Did the public really want to know what I was wearing? I laughed to myself because it was like high school all over again—all this talk about fashion, and me just standing there with no clue about what to contribute to the conversation. This quick thought back to growing up calmed me down just a bit — it was just another ironic reminder of how far I had come. I was able to take a deep breath and reset. Then, I flashed my best smile and answered confidently that I got my outfit from a boutique at the Beverly Center.

DJ Shy getting interviewed at the AX Awards. Photography by Nathaniel Fu

The red carpet was a whole new experience for me — people in my face, clamoring to take my picture. The crowds, the lights, the constant flash bulbs — all of it was a world apart from sitting in an office, listening to KIIS FM on a black transistor radio. It was a night to remember.

My new schedule quickly took shape. I would spin for KIIS FM and do club/event gigs on the weekend. During the week, I would attend red carpet events. It was normal to have events during the week in Hollywood. Being a part of the red carpet scene paid immediate dividends for my new business. I found myself the guest of several film festivals, like the International T.V. Festival, promotional events for various magazines like 13 Minutes Magazine, an Asian American women's lifestyle magazine, and a number of fashion shows, like Jeff Sebelia. I made contacts with executives and artists, and that led to gigs spinning for Missy Elliot, YMI Jeans, and The Black Eyed Peas. Because of my increased presence on the red carpet scene, various designers began approaching me to tell me about their clothes. Shoe designer Michael Antonio started sending me boots, dress shoes, heels — all kinds of shoes — in hopes that I would wear them on the red carpet and thereby get my picture taken wearing their designs. I also got sponsorships from top companies like Tokidoki, Reebok, YMI Jeans, and Rock Anthem clothing. I thought it was ironic to see all these pricey clothing companies send free things on a regular basis to someone like me, a person who didn't have much growing up and even shoplifted in high school because I wanted to fit in.

DJ Shy spinning for Missy Elliot

As my profile grew, I started making contacts with a whole new group of promoters. This only increased my profile and my access to the best spinning gigs the city had to offer. It wasn't long before I landed a gig spinning at the 2006 Grammy Awards after-party. The night of the Grammys was one of the most hectic nights of my young career. I was dating an actor at the time, so I attended a web series wrap party for a pilot that he did for Hollywood uber-producer Marshall Herskovitz. Then, I packed up my gear and rushed over to the Cabana Club just off Sunset Boulevard to do the Grammy after-party. It was an amazing evening, with so many stars and industry heavyweights. It was clear to me then that my decision to pursue this career of mine in a serious way was the right decision.

Scott Michael Foster & Karen Beck

In light of all the hustle and bustle of the entertainment business, it's a daily struggle to keep my head on straight. The key to consistent success is to stay focused and don't take your ego or the Hollywood hype too seriously. You have to remember that, in the midst of all the glitz and glamour, it's still a business. You have to be professional and you have to treat everyone with respect. The entertainment business is one big social network. You have to get out there and be able to build as many contacts as possible to get ahead. In a way, you have to think of all the parties and events as a job. My job is to attend to these events, to hustle and meet the people that I need to meet – not to party and get wasted every night.

When I look back at my journey from a small town in Pennsylvania to where I am today, I realize the driving force behind everything I did was my belief that there was something else— something better—out there for me, and that I had the power to pursue it. If I listened to the doubters, the haters, and even my mom, who naturally was just worried about my well-being, I'd probably be stuck in an office somewhere, listening to the radio and *wishing* I had that job. I wouldn't have my dream job, and I probably would be asking myself constantly "What *if...?*" I don't see much use in regretting things in life, and I believe in always moving forward. Ultimately, I'd like to give back by getting my message of self-empowerment out there. I see this as my legacy — a way to use my DJ career as a way to inspire others and to give back to the community. I want to let other people know how they can accomplish their dreams with passion and perseverance. It's never easy, but it's sure as hell worth the fight. All the work that I'm doing, from a Black Eyed Peas gig to this book, is a means towards that end.

Photographed by Eric Ro

This isn't to say that my time doing those other jobs wasn't worth anything. They were all part of the journey. I'm thankful for the all the opportunities I had at the Children's Hospital and the other jobs I held before I made that leap to full-time deejaying. My 8 to 5 gave me security, stability, and the chance to meet countless interesting and inspiring people. I learned the kind of commitment it takes to be a working professional, and I have always tried to apply this ethic to working in the entertainment industry—a world that can be full of flaky people and often thrives on the chaotic.

• •

It's funny how music can bridge between people—black and white, young and old, Americans and the rest of the world. Besides being my business, deejaying taught me much more about people and about how far I'd come since I was an unhappy little Asian girl in a Pennsylvania Amish town. In 2007, I was hired to spin for the Radioactive Energy Drink tour that traveled around the country to the Northwest, the Midwest, and the South.

Nocturnal Tour Bus

I met all kinds of people and visited parts of the country I'd never seen before. Many of the places I visited were composed of predominantly white communities. There weren't too many minorities around, and when we toured through places like Kentucky and Tennessee, I suddenly felt a familiarity to where I grew up in Amish town. But this time around, I didn't feel awkward or outcast; all my various experiences over the years traveling the world have allowed me to change and to grow as a person. I no longer get caught up in judging people who are close-minded about Asian people, particularly Asian women. That's just how these people grew up. There's increasingly more access, more portrayals and images, of Asians in the media today. This access can help to change stereotypes, and I hope I'm a part of this process by virtue of my appearance at clubs all across the country. I hope this book is a part of it too. The more people are exposed to Asians defying stereotypes—whether that's deejaying or playing on pro sports teams or acting on TV—the more people learn that Asian men and women are just as varied as any other people. Whenever I meet strangers, my hope is to simply put forth a good face for minorities and women. What I find is that I usually end up making a connection with all kinds of people who are vastly different than me through the music that I play. Whatever differences we may have, if we get down to talking about music, we make a *real* connection quickly. Race is no longer an issue at all — it's just about the music and nothing else.

Nocturnal girls

• •

I'm not sure what other doors music will open for me in the future, but I do know that my life right now is about using music to touch people in a positive way. Deejaying has allowed me to pursue another one of my passions—community service. A few years ago when I lived in Koreatown, a few of my neighbors saw me carting out my speakers and turntables to the car. They approached me and asked if I was a DJ. One thing led to another, and I started working with the Green Pastures Program and the Korean Youth and Community Center, or KYCC, in Koreatown. I was amazed when I found out more about their youth outreach programs—I'd have flipped if I'd had access to this kind of stuff when I was a kid. Basically, they were using popular culture like hip-hop to reach out to the youth. They had programs that taught kids to spin, to dance, even to MC. I was moved by the fact that so many Korean American kids in L.A. have such limited access to good education and after-school programs, and this was my chance to help them. I saw myself in those kids. So many of them are coming from situations just like mine—growing up in broken homes without a father, trying to find their identity amidst adversity and poverty. Not all Asian American kids can be lumped into the "model minority" stereotype. We're not all straight-A math geniuses, always quiet and seeking approval. Many of us grew up in broken homes with single moms, even foster and adoptive parents, never truly understanding anything about our heritage, let alone who we really are as individuals.

L.A. can be a sea of distractions for kids growing up here; there are too many opportunities to get into trouble, no matter what race they happen to be. These things didn't exist for me growing up in Amish town, and I can honestly say that is what saved me. I was also lucky to realize my passion for music early on, which kept me out of trouble, at least most of the time. Too many kids in L.A. aren't able to connect with their own passions and hopes because of all the distractions that can be found out on the city's dangerous streets: gangs, teen pregnancy, drinking, drugs, and violence. I saw all this when I volunteered to teach kids at KYCC to deejay, and I realized that there was so much more that I could do. I soon became involved in the Step Up Women's Network, an organization that specifically targets young girls who are at risk of falling into gang life. I forged a friendship with a young girl rather quickly and became her mentor. I showed her all I could about the art of spinning. And now? She wants to be a DJ herself!

Karen mentoring at Step Up Womens Network. Photo taken by Amy Bojanowski

Being a mentor is such an incredible experience. Having the ability to have a positive influence on someone's life, on a real and personal level, is something you simply can't duplicate. Sure, the red carpets and the celebrity parties are exciting and fun—but nothing beats the good feeling you get from helping other people achieve what they want in life. Girls like her are at an age where they are open to almost anything—the good and the bad. And too often, in certain cities like Los Angeles, it's usually the bad that wins out. I see so much potential in the quiet girl who is waiting to see which road she'll take, and I feel so much sadness when no one takes her hand to show her the right way. Like me, she finds herself growing up without anyone to guide her. I'm lucky enough to have found the right path for myself for now, but what about all those kids who weren't so lucky? Music has given me the opportunity to reach out to them, one on one. And in the end, maybe that's what lies at the core of what I keep pushing myself to do. Deejaying is a job, but it's also an open door that can lead to influence and real change.

I truly believe in the power of positive thought. I believe in mind over matter, and that positive energy moves in circles. Whatever you put out there into the world, you really do get back. I have seen this so many times in my relatively short life and career to know that there is something to it. As long as I believed in myself and followed my heart, I knew there was nothing that I could not do. That meant defying stereotypes. That meant traveling the world as a DJ. That meant getting my dream job at the number one radio station in the country. And yes, that meant helping others just like me follow their hearts too. A Korean American girl with a humble upbringing from a broken home can still move people with music. I held on to that belief and never looked back.

ABOUT THE AUTHOR

Photographed by Michael Robert Hartman

Karen Jin Beck, aka DJ Shy was the first female on-air mixer at the No. 1 Top 40 radio station in America, 102.7 KIIS-FM in Los Angeles. This Clear Channel station with over 2.6 million listeners each week features Ryan Seacrest as the morning host.

As the headlining DJ for Singapore's famous New Years Eve party at Siloso beach, Shy is used to performing in front of crowds of 20,000 fans at some of the finest clubs in the world, from L.A. to Asia and back. These clubs include Q Bar in Bangkok and Ministry of Sound.

In addition to spinning in front of large crowds, DJ Shy is certainly not camera shy. She graces the screen with guest starring roles on CBS "The Bold and the Beautiful," MTV's "Daddy's Girls", STYLE Networks's "Mel B: It's a Scary World", and Disney Channel's "Totally Suite New Years Eve." She also made cameos in Sundance Film "Sympathy for Delicious" starring Orlando Bloom, an award winning indie film "Go For It", and "Battle B-Boy" which features the group FM. Lastly, you may find her in music videos such as Cascada's "What Hurts the Most" and Darren Styles "Girls Like You."

Shy got her start at the world famous Laugh Factory comedy club in Hollywood, where she spun at sold-out shows for comics like Norm MacDonald, Damon and Marlon Wayans, George Lopez, Chris Rock, Bob Saget, Dane Cook, Dave Chapelle, Roger Dangerfield and others. She spins Top 40, 80s, pop, rock, house, hip-hop, R&B and reggae music.